Now You Are God's People

Now You Are God's People

*Reflections on 1 Peter for
God's Church in God's World*

Justin Welby
Jennifer Strawbridge
Abigail Harries Martin

scm press

Published in 2024 by SCM Press
Editorial office
3rd Floor, Invicta House,
110 Golden Lane,
London EC1Y 0TG, UK

www.scmpress.co.uk

SCM Press is an imprint of Hymns Ancient & Modern Ltd
(a registered charity)

Hymns Ancient & Modern® is a registered trademark of
Hymns Ancient & Modern Ltd
13A Hellesdon Park Road, Norwich,
Norfolk NR6 5DR, UK

British Library Cataloguing in Publication data

A catalogue record for this book is available from the British Library

ISBN 978-0-334-06564-7

Typeset by Regent Typesetting

Contents

Introduction

JENNIFER STRAWBRIDGE AND
ABIGAIL HARRIES MARTIN

The first letter of Peter is written to communities who, empowered by the Spirit, are called to witness to the transforming joy of Christ, even as they suffer for Christ's name. It raises an utterly compelling and inspiring vision of God's kingdom. Written to a Christian diaspora – a group of people different from the society around them as a result of their conversion to faith in Christ – the audience of 1 Peter are suffering as rejected outsiders in their own civil communities. Within this context, the apostolic author offers encouragement for unity over division and for humility over anxiety. It speaks about belonging, alienation, slavery and persecution – words in which you can immediately hear the echoes in our world today. As the following reflections engage with the five chapters of 1 Peter, we find time and again that unity in Christ draws us together amid division, calling all Christians to witness, to hope and to holiness as God's united people, serving one God for one purpose.

The chapters that follow are expositions of 1 Peter for the church today in dialogue with voices from across the globe. The book begins with five chapters, a convenient number since 1 Peter contains five chapters. However, the chapter divisions of 1 Peter are not always helpful (and were only introduced in the 1500s). This is especially true for 1 Peter 2 and 1 Peter 3, where the letter calls various sectors of the Church to 'accept the authority of' (see 1 Pet. 2.13, 2.18, 3.1). The content of each chapter was initially offered by the Archbishop of Canterbury at the 2022 Lambeth Conference – a gathering of bishops, spouses and guests from across the Anglican Communion that takes place approximately once every decade.

Each reflection is the product of years of conversations that began at the 2018 St Augustine Seminar – a gathering of 35 scholars from across the globe – and continued through focused conversations with Archbishop Justin Welby in the two years leading up to the conference. The reflections draw together the transcripts of the reflections as delivered by Archbishop Justin. We are especially grateful for the expert editorial and transcription work of Emma Barnes. These reflections introduce key themes from 1 Peter, draw out questions and challenges from 1 Peter for today's church and world, and ultimately explore how 1 Peter continues to speak to readers 2000 years after the letter was composed.

Within many of the reflections, readers will also encounter excurses on key words and phrases from 1 Peter such as suffering, holiness and hope, and how such words are understood in different communities. Because many of these words from 1 Peter are understood differently in different contexts, the voices from more than twenty countries add depth and breadth to how we understand 1 Peter within a global community. Within three of the chapters, we also find longer reflections on themes of hospitality, suffering, holiness and roaring lions from Christians in Mozambique, the United States, Malaysia, the Democratic Republic of the Congo, Pakistan, New Zealand and Kenya.

This book concludes with five short reflections on 1 Peter written in homiletic form from biblical scholars based in the United Kingdom, Brazil, Kenya and India. These short reflections, which may be especially helpful to those preaching and leading biblical reflections in the years when 1 Peter is part of the lectionary cycle, are introduced more fully below.

Each chapter concludes with a Bible study, created by members of the St Augustine's Seminar. These studies draw on the voices, stories, struggles and prayers of scholars from six continents and represent a range of Christian traditions and experiences. They are offered for all who wish to dive deeper into the book of 1 Peter within their own setting, whether in a group or in personal prayer. There are no 'right' answers to the questions. Rather, we hope that all engaged in these studies on 1 Peter will find and create space where what is on the heart can be spoken, where Holy Scripture can be encountered, and where you may be open to what the Holy Spirit might speak through Scripture.

This suite of resources – biblical expositions and reflections by Archbishop Justin, Bible studies, and short reflections by scholars from different cultures and contexts – may be used on their own to support study of 1 Peter. They may also be used with the commentary on 1 Peter produced by the St Augustine Seminar members, also available from SCM Press: *The First Letter of Peter: A Global Commentary* (2020). Finally, films were produced about 1 Peter, with discussion of each chapter and difficult questions raised by this text for the church and world today.[1]

Those whose voices are represented in this book have had profound encounters with one another as we have engaged with 1 Peter. Our hope is that through your study of 1 Peter, you might find deeper engagement with God's Word and deeper love for God's world. May each of us come to 1 Peter with humble hearts and open spirits, that God's Spirit may guide us together. May we not weary in seeking God's presence, because God does not weary in coming to us and transforming us.

---

1 https://www.lambethconference.org/phase-1/watch-the-1-peter-videos/ (accessed 7.9.2023).

Called into Hope and Holiness in Christ

1 *Peter* 1

Why 1 Peter? When we started looking at 1 Peter as the biblical foundation of the Lambeth Conference in 2022,[1] almost everyone said: '1 Peter? Why 1 Peter? What's wrong with Paul? Is he out of fashion?' But once they studied 1 Peter, they said: 'Yes, 1 Peter, obviously.'

The Bible is central, foundational, to all that we do together as Christians. Anglicans, among many other traditions and denominations, are a people catholic and reformed, devoted to Holy Scripture. Studying Scripture together, hearing Scripture in our liturgies, wrestling with the text together and listening to the Spirit, in the Anglican tradition, is not the privilege of some but is open to all. It is the gift of God's Word to every Christian.

1 Peter engages a number of big themes for us as a church: holiness, exile and displacement, power and authority, hope and suffering, hospitality and others. It is striking that, although the world in which we live is completely different to that of Peter in the first century, and although the world has shifted on its axis in the last ten years because of Covid, climate crisis, wars

---

1 Convened by the Archbishop of Canterbury, the Lambeth Conference is an international meeting of Anglican bishops. The 2022 Lambeth Conference met in Canterbury, UK, and explored what it means to be God's church for God's world.

and acts of terror, the message and context of 1 Peter are still very relevant.

From its very opening, we are told that the letter is from the Apostle Peter and written to the exiles of the dispersion, the diaspora, who are spread throughout Asia Minor. Exile has two meanings at the opening of 1 Peter. Exile means, first, that the Christians addressed in this letter had left their homeland to live as strangers and foreigners in Asia Minor. Secondly, exile is a theological term, meaning that all Christians everywhere, no matter their political or geographical context, are living in exile, separated from their eternal home in heaven. From the beginning, Peter's communities suffered from rejection and harassment by the society around them, because their Christian identity made them suspect. It was suspicious and unusual that, when Christians gathered together, for example, enslaved persons, aristocrats, foreigners and people of various backgrounds, all shared in the Eucharist. 1 Peter demonstrates, therefore, that when we are faithful, we will find we are exiles.

The letter of 1 Peter demonstrates life under a system opposed to the faith and, in that context, how to be faithful and how to survive. This tension runs throughout the letter, but instead of being excluded and shunned, those called the 'exiles' are identified by Peter as 'chosen', 'destined' and 'sanctified' by Jesus Christ. They are exiles and yet they are chosen; they are suffering and yet they have a foundation for hope: Jesus Christ. This identity is central to the letter. God has chosen these exiles as his own, and the Spirit has made these exiles holy. They are called to be pilgrims and to follow Jesus Christ.

1 Peter is, in many places, a text that, to many of our ears, is startling. Many things in 1 Peter are difficult for our ears to hear; slavery, migration, social identity, exclusion and suffering are in our face in an uncomfortable way. These chapters intend to challenge us in what it means to be faithful to the text and to be faithful to what it teaches us, because 1 Peter has a richness and depth that has much to teach us if we are open to it. It also has an utterly compelling message concerning the call to proclaim the transforming joy of Jesus Christ, to embody a living

hope, to be living stones, to enact constant, mutual love and to be transformed by God's Word which is 'good news' – these are the imperatives of 1 Peter.

For many of us, 1 Peter touches on difficult topics, and we are not going to skip them; across each of these chapters you will hear a number of voices engaging with Scripture, talking about these difficult issues. Through the excurses across each exposition, we will learn to listen to each other and to hear and learn how different communities have different understandings of key themes in 1 Peter. These excurses, with voices from across the globe, also enable empathy for contexts and challenges that many of us cannot begin to understand.

1 Peter calls us to gentleness and humility. Having a spirit of honesty, encouragement, gentleness and humility is the only way we can walk and witness together. All too often we are not direct and we prefer to divide and control, but that is not the way of 1 Peter. We are going to face some tough issues across these chapters, but Peter gives us tools with which to remain faithful to Christ and to one another. This letter speaks directly about our call as God's one holy people, challenges us to hope and mutual love, sets before us a vision of reconciliation, and returns time and again to Christ as the source of hope, holiness, comfort and leadership. We are called to be guardians and teachers, and our foundation in this is Christ and Christ's word. Every element of Peter's letter, every element of his call to serve God's people and what that might look like, is grounded in Christ just as we are called to be grounded in Christ. The dynamic action of God in Christ is our foundation.

Introduction of 1 Peter 1

1 Peter 1 sets the tone for the whole letter. Those called 'exiles' in 1 Peter 1.2 are immediately identified by Peter as 'chosen', 'destined' and 'sanctified' by Jesus Christ. They are the communities of 1 Peter; they have experienced or they are experiencing persecution. Peter exhorts Christians in the diaspora, in an

environment of despair, suspicion and hostility, to put their faith in God and not lose hope.

One of the challenges of 1 Peter is how it expresses truth and encouragement to those who are persecuted and who live in danger because of their faith. There are many Christians across our globe who live in places of persecution, some of it violent and open, some of it slightly better concealed. It is difficult for those who are not persecuted to understand the reality of the recipients of this letter. There is potential for disconnect and judgement, of judging Peter for what he writes without considering his context, but we are not to judge Peter for what he writes. We are to listen and to apply hermeneutical skills to understand what this means for us today. Here the theme of alienation comes to the fore, which has been exasperated by the pandemic, wars, social division and political division. In an excursus below, voices from around the globe are engaged on the meaning of alienation in today's world.

Hope is the second theme of 1 Peter. Hope cannot be separated in 1 Peter from the life that Jesus offers in his death and resurrection. Hope in Christ is not the same as optimism. There was once a minister in Northern Ireland during the Troubles – the fighting in Northern Ireland – whom journalists would ask after meetings: 'Minister, are you optimistic?' He would respond: 'No, but I am hopeful.' He was a Christian and understood the difference. Hope is not what we have, but rather it is what God has for us. Hope is not based on wishful thinking or fantasy. It is not based on propaganda promoted by the (Roman) Empire, or those pretending to have God's authority. Hope is instead secure and anchored in God, meaning that hope can confront death and despair only when it is based on the death and resurrection of Christ. Hope is not based on our own actions or our personal piety, but has everything to do with who Jesus is and what Jesus has done. There is no hope except in Christ.

Many in our world have to struggle to hold on to hope: hope for justice, hope for the ability to meet basic human needs, hope for the land and water lost to the changing climate, hope amid storms and cyclones that strike, and hope for an end to war, gender- and race-based violence and persecution. I heard from a fellow bishop recently that, in the province they lead, they serve and lead people who are drifting away, in some cases from the church, as a result of 15 years of war. Those drifting away are saying, after so many years of war, 'We pray, but there is still war. How can we still hope?' The answer is the hope in the life and death of Jesus Christ.

Rebirth and resurrection is the third theme of 1 Peter. The movement from death to life, for us, is connected to the resurrection of Christ and the calling of Peter's community as God's own people. We have life now and we hope for eternal life only because of Jesus. There is new life because they are God's people. This rebirth in Christ moves us from no hope to hope, from ignorance to knowledge and from disobedience to obedience.

Knowing joy in the midst of suffering is 1 Peter's fourth theme. Personally, I find this one of the hardest things with which to engage, because we all have different personalities. Difficult as it may sound, the author calls his communities to rejoice and specifically to know Christ's joy in the midst of suffering, because joy in Christ is something else.

Some years ago, I met a cardinal, Cardinal Văn Thuận, in Switzerland. He was Archbishop of Saigon – what is now Ho Chi Minh City – in South Vietnam when I met him. When the Communists took over in 1975, he was arrested and held for nine years in solitary confinement, where he wrote extensively about hope and joy. When I met him, he spoke of his experience of nine years of torture; of how his torturer had become a Christian and ended up in prison with him; of how he had started a seminary in the prison and how the lectures were given by whispering down the line when the prisoners were being counted; and he told of how, in his prison, in his cell by himself underground, he said Mass every day, with one grain of rice and just enough rice wine to hold in the palm of his hand, which was the chalice. As he said the Mass he danced with joy, because he was focused on Christ.

With a focus on Christ, those suffering now are assured of the work of God to bring new life in which the past is forgiven, the present is protected and the future is assured. Christ's suffering and glory serve as the example and encouragement to these exiled Christians of 1 Peter. Christ's suffering and self-sacrifice are the foundations of the fifth theme in 1 Peter, which is the call to holiness of those who bear Christ's name. The call to holiness is a call to imitate God in God's self-sacrificial movement towards the other and us in Jesus Christ. God is holy and so we too are called to be holy and this holiness is not something we can control or earn. It is an invitation and a gift.

This leads us to the final theme of the letter, that of inheritance and gift. As 1 Peter assures us, God's gifts are better than gold or silver. They never perish, spoil or fade. They are the one thing like that; they are the only things we carry with us beyond the grave. When we stand before Christ, facing judgement, our Lord and Saviour will want to know: 'Do you love me? Did you say Jesus is Lord?' While holiness, hope and being chosen as God's own people are all gifts from God, the ultimate gift described in 1 Peter 1 is the gift of salvation in Jesus Christ.

There is also a sense of journey and growth across 1 Peter. In many parts of our world, and in many parts of the church, there is a sense that once you're converted, then that's it. Peter, however, gives us a sense of movement, of continued growth and development. His theme was picked up in the early church, particularly in the writings of Irenaeus and Origen, who said that formation was always a journey and that the point of conversion was one of the most dangerous moments of the faith (alongside persecution) as it was then that temptation to give up was the greatest. Conversion was a moment of danger as a new convert was revealed and exposed to new threats and needed to be built up and supported by their community especially in situations of suffering.

One of the challenges of 1 Peter, therefore, is to ask how we draw people into continual growth in Christ throughout their lives. This is our calling as bishops, as Christians: that we don't just see those around us make a commitment to Christ, but help them to grow deeper and stronger in their faith. It is worth noting that many of the verbs in 1 Peter in the Greek are active verbs. They assume an action is ongoing and not a one-time thing: *becoming* living stones, *becoming* examples to our flocks and *casting* our anxieties onto God.

The gifts of new life patterned on the witness of Jesus are indeed both openly inclusive, welcoming *everyone* as they are, and yet radically transformative, leaving no-one just as they are. Hope in Christ transforms our fears and desires. Hope and holiness are linked in an inalienable embrace: to set one's hope on Christ is in every aspect of life to become holy as he is holy, which also continually entails sobering up, being steady and 'preparing our minds for action' (1 Pet. 1.13).

We are united in our hope, in our love for Jesus Christ, but we are also divided by our assumptions that the key themes of 1 Peter mean the same for everyone else as they do for us, or that my suffering is exactly the same as your suffering. But this is simply not the case, and that is why we must come together, listen to one another, walk with one another and learn from one another, because the same words mean different things to different people.

Empathy, walking in one another's shoes, is much harder than judgement (if we are called to judge at all – that seems to be God's job, not ours), but we are called precisely to empathy. It is easy to condemn, but it is hard to tell the story of someone with whom we disagree in such a way that they recognize it as their story. How can we walk and witness together if we do not know each other's stories? Many words could be chosen to exemplify our need to listen, learn from and stand with one another, but let's begin with one, the word 'hope', and look at how hope is represented around our world.

Excursus: Voices on Hope[2]

In my context, hope is:

✧ a situation where we long for a united and prosperous Zimbabwe, where we see each other as created in the image of God (Zimbabwe);

✧ a heavenly blessing that keeps us hanging on to life … without having or embracing such hope, a hope for a better future, we will perish and wither (Syria/Lebanon);

✧ believing in those things that are yet unseen (Pakistan);

✧ dóchas, which is the Irish word for hope. It means the hope that depends on and derives from trust. When people truly trust each other, and sometimes with difficulty build trust, then the atmosphere emerges where there can be understanding and progress and hope (Ireland);

✧ the right vision for the right future, especially for young people (Israel);

✧ something I know that, however long it may take, it's going to come to pass and so, I'm willing to wait for it (Nigeria);

✧ knowing and seeing how the church has grown (Sri Lanka);

✧ a ray of light in the darkness (India);

✧ trusting that God sees a bigger, wider, longer view than I can ever imagine (United Kingdom);

✧ my dream of a life where all can flourish, where women and girls confidently expect an early end to all forms of conflict and violence, so they can live fruitful lives, fulfilling lives, lives free from fear, abuse and discrimination (Guyana);

---

2 Each excursus contains short statements initially gathered together in video format which have been transcribed for this book by Emma Barnes. The statements are drawn from leaders, lay and ordained, from across the globe. Their location by country is noted at the end of each short reflection.

✧ reconciliation. It is reconciliation between the north and the south of the island, which has remained divided since 1974 (Cyprus);

✧ be[ing] confident that things will be better in the future, being confident that God is there, and that injustice will not last forever, occupation will not last forever, the violation of human and natural rights will not last forever. The last word is for God, not for evil. The last word is for justice and peace, not for war (Palestine/Jordan);

✧ looking for a better place where there is peace and where there is love and where there is quality education and people are living in harmony (South Sudan);

✧ the fact that God is in control, that God has the last word, not humans, not states, not governments. No one has the last word. God has the last word (Palestine);

✧ it's envisioning to witness love and unity among Indians, irrespective of one's religion and like different cultures (India);

✧ [the belief that,] despite the situation that we have currently in South Sudan, God is walking with us and he is guiding us in each step of the way, because his promises never fail (South Sudan/United Kingdom);

✧ that one day, [the] Pakistani Church will be like Christ. It can become a joy, blessing and a healing for the total Pakistan (Pakistan);

✧ being able to trust God in all times and circumstances (Argentina);

✧ despite what you might be experiencing at that point in time, seeing that there is still something beautiful that can happen, that there's still something waiting for you in the end, in a way that you mightn't even expect it. For me, that is hope (Trinidad).

The Person of Peter

That these themes of hope, suffering, joy, despair, holiness, exile and transformation are all attributed to the Apostle Peter cannot be a coincidence or mistake. Peter's story embodies these themes. The same Peter who denied Christ is the one commissioned, forgiven and called to 'tend the flock', just as those not a people are a people. Peter is also a model of lived suffering. He knows about alienation and the longing we have to belong. Jesus called Peter to follow him in his ministry, and Peter volunteered to do so. But he failed, and ended up denying Jesus three times. Peter suffered from isolation and alienation as he separated himself from Christ when questioned about his relationship with Christ. By denying him, Peter struggled with what it meant to follow Christ. If we return to John chapter 13, we find Peter struggling: 'What? Wash my feet? You'll never wash my feet!' And Jesus says: 'If you want to belong to me, I must wash your feet.' And yet the same Peter who denied Christ is the one commissioned and forgiven.

We know Peter before the resurrection, a Peter who suffers, who judged, who failed, who lacked understanding and who saw at least one of his fellow disciples – the Beloved Disciple – not as a brother in Christ, but as a competitor. But we also know Peter after the resurrection, the first one called by Christ to 'tend the flock'. He offers us a model of lived suffering, embodying both the suffering of being separated from Christ and the ultimate suffering of death for following and proclaiming Christ.

In his life and in his death, Peter is one who knows about alienation and the longing we have to be one with Christ. The story of 1 Peter tells us something of Peter's story, but it also speaks directly to our stories. We, too, are like Peter. We suffer, we judge, we compete and we fail to follow Christ faithfully. And yet we are called by Christ to tend the flock of God. 1 Peter upsets power dynamics and calls us to listen to those whose experiences in our world today are much closer to those of the communities of 1 Peter. It is indeed striking how many Christians across our world today say that 1 Peter seems to be written for them: Bishop Azad from Pakistan and Archbishop Hosam from Jerusalem, for example. For as much as we are called to hope, hope and suffering are opposite sides of the same coin in 1 Peter. Let us engage other global voices telling us what alienation means for them in their context today.

Excursus: Voices on Alienation

In my context, alienation is:

✧ making an assumption about a specific person because you think you know them better than you really do (Trinidad);

✧ I think of me as an alien in a foreign country, because that's where I am (United States);

✧ being indifferent to the needs of nature, being intolerant to the diversities of communities that exist (Peru);

✧ actually not knowing love (Sri Lanka);

✧ being judged, being discriminated against because of my tribal grouping and region. It means being excluded because I'm regarded as not good enough and therefore cannot qualify for certain privileges (Zambia);

✧ not being seen, not feeling like you're seen or known or loved. It's really hard when you don't have anybody to share bad news with, but actually when you don't even have anybody to share good news with, I think that's really what alienation is (United Kingdom);

✧ [something that] has a nuance of deprivation. And in my context as a Ghanaian, we have many young people who are alienated from social life due to unemployment (Ghana);

✧ [when] you can see that I'm an Indian, but I don't look like an Indian; I don't have those typical Indian features. Me – along with so many other Nagas and Northeast people – we're often mistaken to be Southeast Asians, and I think we are most discriminated [against] because of how we look (India);

✧ [when] I once went through a very deep, dark period of alienation and it felt like I was at the bottom of a very dark well, where even God was a long way up and nobody really understood where I'd gone (United Kingdom);

✧ that there's a sense in which for a long time we've been alienated from the resources that are around us, alienated from each other, alienated by conflict and by greed and by corruption in many things, and what we experience is poverty, all over and around us (Zimbabwe);

✧ [how,] in my country, Dalit people feel that they are alienated and forbidden to participate in some ritual, religious and cultural activities. Dalits, referring to the outcast and scheduled caste people, [are] about 25% [of] India's population. 1.3 billion people are Dalits (India);

✧ [when] I got saved at a very young age, and it got to a point my aunties were isolating me for my faith, like 'Oh you're saved', and they're like, 'If you're saved you're going to be poor, you know', and so I felt very lonely, alienated because of my faith at that point, but that didn't stop me; I still continue trusting in God (Kenya);

✧ [the] bitter experiences of alienation as a woman presbyter, a priest. The male-dominated clergy in the diocese alienated me from all the diocese and committees for over 20 years, but the Lord has lifted me up as the bishop of the same diocese (India);

✧ that, because I was a Christian and I would stand my ground [against] a lot [of people] participating in corruption, a lot [of people] participating in fraudulent acts, I would definitely get left out. They would look at me as a Christian and say, 'She's not going to allow this to pass through her, so let's keep her down' (Nigeria);

✧ when you start feeling that you're a refugee within your own country, and you feel that you are just [an] internally displaced person and start thinking as if you are a second- or third-class citizen within your country. Then it becomes very difficult, very difficult, for survival, you know, because it psychologically kills you (Pakistan).

Conclusion

These conversations reveal such different understandings, all based in Scripture or experience, of the words 'hope' and 'alienation'. Here in the Global North we continually need to remind ourselves that the Bible was written over a millennium, across huge differences in circumstances, by people inspired by the Spirit of God. And when it is read in different circumstances, people hear words in their own language; they hear them in different ways.

We need 1 Peter at this time because we need each other. We aren't perfect, but we are called to walk together, to witness together and to listen together in Christ. Many in our world today are alienated like the communities of 1 Peter, and we are called to listen to and support them. We will see when we get to 1 Peter 5 that Peter calls us to solidarity with brothers and sisters in Christ, across the innumerable understandings and experiences of exile and alienation in our world. 1 Peter calls his communities, who are exiles and who are aliens, to live as 'God's chosen people'; those who are excluded, marginalized and unheard are God's people. We are God's people called to embrace our common call to hope in our Lord and Saviour Jesus Christ, but we are undeniably divided. Those who are included or excluded from our communities, those who are the aliens and the exiles, differs from region to region, community to community. How we think about hope differs as well, as we have seen.

I am convinced that with any of these key themes – holiness, suffering, persecution, rebirth, salvation, hospitality – we will find disagreement, and yet this division is not the good news. This is not the gospel. Peter ends the first chapter by telling us that the message shared is the good news, which is the foundation of our hope and of our life together. The death and resurrection of Jesus is *the* foundation of the living hope to which Peter calls his community and this enables us to stand firm against all that brings death in individual lives and communities in the world. The gospel of Christ that we proclaim, the hope that we embody, is good news, not just for us, but for all God's people. The good news is also that *oneness in Christ robs all divisions of power*. Oneness in Christ robs all that seeks to kill us of power.

The power of Christ overcomes all that seeks to alienate, to fragment and to cause fear. We may be disparate and we may be divided, but we have a common identity that is fundamentally above all and that transcends all: our identity in Christ. Christ is our common identity, for every single person reading this text. Our mission is God's mission. Our hope is living and alive, not stagnant and stale. What is the good news in your context? How might you be open to encountering the good news of Jesus Christ?

1 Peter 1 ends with a call to mutual love, because this is the key to witness: 'have genuine mutual love, love one another deeply from the heart' (1.22). Mutual love is central to what it is to be a witness of Christ. This letter is addressed to the Christian community *continually growing* in love. The call to 'love one another deeply from the heart' is the focus at the end of this first chapter, and it is the key, the most important

response that the saving act of God in Christ requires. They will know we are Christians by our love. Do those in our world know that we are Christians by our love for one another? I wouldn't guess it from what I have experienced and seen. We cannot proclaim the good news of God's love with or to those we hate and revile. Why is it so difficult to love all believers or all people in our wider communities? What holds us back from loving one another 'deeply from the heart'?

Questions for Bible Study

Hope: 1 Peter 1.3–5: 'Blessed be the God and Father of our Lord Jesus Christ! By his great mercy he has given us a new birth into a living hope through the resurrection of Jesus Christ from the dead, and into an inheritance that is imperishable, undefiled and unfading, kept in heaven for you, who are being protected by the power of God through faith for a salvation ready to be revealed in the last time.'

Reflect on one or both of the following questions:
✧ 1 Peter speaks about God giving us 'new birth into a living hope'. What does 'living hope' mean to you?
✧ What does it mean to your church or community?

Holiness: 1 Peter 1.13–16: 'Therefore prepare your minds for action; discipline yourselves; set all your hope on the grace that Jesus Christ will bring you when he is revealed. Like obedient children, do not be conformed to the desires that you formerly had in ignorance. Instead, as he who called you is holy, be holy yourselves in all your conduct; for it is written, "You shall be holy, for I am holy."'

Reflect on one or more of the following questions:

✧ Five commands appear in 1 Peter 1.13–16 above: prepare your minds for action; discipline yourselves; set all your hope on the grace given by Jesus Christ; do not be conformed to the desires that you formerly had; be holy in all your conduct.

✧ Which of these commands do you most need to put into practice?

✧ What does being holy mean for you?

✧ Do you struggle with being made holy? If so, in what ways?

✧ How do you experience God making you or your community holy?

Mutual Love: 1 Peter 1.21–22: 'Through him you have come to trust in God, who raised him from the dead and gave him glory, so that your faith and hope are set on God. Now that you have purified your souls by your obedience to the truth so that you have genuine mutual love, love one another deeply from the heart.'

Reflect on these questions:

✧ Why is it difficult to love all believers or all people in your wider community?

✧ What holds you back from loving 'one another deeply from the heart'?

2

A Holy People Following Christ

1 Peter 2.1–12

Within this chapter, we will follow a conversation between three bishops from very different contexts: Bishop Steven Abbarrow from West Malaysia, Bishop Phoebe Roaf from West Tennessee, and Bishop Manuel Ernesto from Nampula, West Mozambique, on what it means to be God's holy people in God's world today. We begin with each bishop introducing themselves and their contexts.

Discussion Part One: Contexts

Bishop Stephen Abbarrow is from the Province of Southeast Asia and the Diocesan Bishop of the Diocese of West Malaysia. He has been a bishop for slightly more than a year. He speaks of encouraging his diocese in the context of several difficulties: emerging from the Covid pandemic and seeing the virus become endemic; grappling with falling income rates; political, religious and social instability; and a very militant atmosphere. He asks a question that he says has 'been a focal point' in his diocese: 'How do we continue to focus on discipleship, on leadership development and church planting and caring for not only ourselves, but our neighbours as well?' He asks further, 'How do we continue to be holy in spite of all these challenges?'

Bishop Phoebe Roaf is the Diocesan Bishop for the Diocese of West Tennessee. Her cathedral and office are not very far from the location where Dr Martin Luther King Jr was murdered in 1968, which reminds her that the question of respect for people of all races is really huge in the southern part of the United States, where the institution of slavery was quite firmly established for many years. There is a great need for increased relationships among people of very diverse backgrounds. She speaks of how she has been a bishop for three years, but she still feels like a 'baby'. It is a challenge to learn what it means to be a leader in these really turbulent times with so much uncertainty, and yet she thinks this turbulence gives the church a real opportunity to be the church. She is excited about the possibilities, even though she acknowledges there are aspects of this call to leadership that can be really difficult. Nevertheless, this call has also been life-affirming for Bishop Phoebe.

Bishop Manuel Ernesto is the Bishop of the Anglican Diocese of Nampula, which is a new diocese in Mozambique created in 2019. Bishop Manuel is based in northern Mozambique, in the province of Nampula, but with more responsibilities up to the Tanzanian border. His diocese is located in a predominantly Muslim area. He is glad to participate in this global conversation on faith, and identifies three challenges in his diocese, the first of which is conflict. He describes the militant situation in Mozambique, where terrorists and unknown armed groups have been a threat since 2017. So far, he says, there are more than one million internally displaced people because of this conflict. His diocese is also facing challenges, as in any part of the world, with the Covid pandemic. The pandemic was very difficult in Mozambique because the entire economic system was under pressure and people lost their jobs.

Bishop Manuel says that nearly everything has to be rebuilt. The third challenge he identifies is climate change. His diocese is often hit by cyclones. At the time of this interview in mid-2022, they had seen three cyclones since Christmas the previous year and were trying to recover. Despite these challenges, Bishop Manuel says that his diocese is one of great joy. They are happy to have people with great faith and with vibrant and new churches being born in the diocese, and they are also happy to have a lot of young people. Mozambique has about 30 million inhabitants, half of whom are under the age of 15. He speaks of the challenge to transmit the gospel to this new generation, and wonders how many of these young people will follow Christ through the Anglican family.

Exposition of 1 Peter 2.1–12

Our panellists deliberately represent radically different contexts. The question they are all asking comes directly from 1 Peter 2.1–12: how can we be and continue to be holy in light of the challenges we face? Holiness and the call to be holy are central themes in 1 Peter and in 1 Peter 2 in particular. Before Peter can return to this call to holiness, however, he begins to unpack some of the consequences of living in Christ and being a Christian. In 1 Peter 1, believers are called to faith and hope and are given a new identity in Christ as God's chosen people. Now, in 1 Peter 2, Peter begins to unfold for his hearers and readers just what this means for their daily lives.

1 Peter 2 begins with a warning against all that undermines the unity of the community and the mutual love that they are to show for one another. Peter speaks of avoiding guile, malice, envy, slander and insincerity, and that abandoning these things is the consequence of loving one another and being born anew

in Christ. 1 Peter 2 thus starts with the things that separate us from God, a number of which we have seen during Covid: envy, greed and hoarding, for example. A pillar of Peter's ethics is not harbouring hatred or acting with guile or hypocrisy toward those with whom we disagree.

From the start, 1 Peter 2 continues focusing on the identity of his communities in Christ. He then expands on this identity by introducing the language of the 'living stone'. Jesus is described with that title (2.4), and those who believe in Jesus, Christians, are given that title as well (2.5). In the Holy Land and Palestine, especially, Christians call themselves 'living stones', because, while people might go to the Holy Land to see the ancient stones that are 'dead', Christians are the living stones, who are so often overlooked and ignored by the pilgrims, and who endure persecution, especially with occupation.

The language of 'living' in chapter 2, therefore, applies not only to our hope, which lives and is prepared for us, or to God's living word, as in 1 Peter 1, but also to God's people and to Christ. Living stones are those stones that are not yet quarried. They are still growing, being shaped by the elements and acquiring sediment. The imagery of the stone comes from the Old Testament. It is found in Isaiah 8.14 and 28.16, and in Psalm 118.22. As elsewhere in the New Testament, the author of this text draws on the Old Testament and interprets it in the light of the church's experience of faith in Jesus Christ. Believers in Jesus inherit the calling and join in the calling that God gave to Israel to be 'a chosen race, a royal priesthood, a holy nation, God's own people' (2.9).

Directly connected to this call to be a living stone and to love one another is the call for believers in Jesus to 'proclaim the mighty acts of God who called [them] out of darkness into his marvellous light' (2.9). Even in the face of hostility and persecution, 1 Peter insists believers should strive to live in such a way that the unbelievers among whom they reside may 'see [their] honourable deeds and glorify God when he comes to judge' (2.12). Peter recognizes that this will not be easy. On the one hand, just as Jesus was rejected, Peter's listeners must not be surprised that they are being rejected. However, Jesus, the 'stone that the builders rejected, has become the very head of the corner' (Ps. 118.22; Matt. 21.42), and those who do not believe in this 'cornerstone' will stumble and fall.

Peter continues with a message of hope: his community should feel heartened that they will be vindicated in the last days, because Jesus Christ has already been vindicated by God through the resurrection. In spite of opposition from society, Peter's community should find a sense of self-worth, because they are the 'chosen' just as Christ is the 'chosen one'. It is at this point that 1 Peter identifies holiness as a central aspect of our calling, for God is holy and God's people are called to be holy in all their conduct, to be a holy priesthood and a holy nation. The vocation, the call, of everyone is to holiness and to God. But how we understand 'holiness' and what we mean by 'holy' differs depending on our context and experiences. Let's turn to some reflections on holiness and engage with how this call to holiness in 1 Peter 2 is understood by Christians across our world.

Excursus: Voices on Holiness

In my context, holiness is:

✧ [when] I think of God as being holy. God is consistently and unchangingly good, faithful, just, righteous and so on (Sri Lanka);

✧ the wooing – it's a rather old-fashioned word – the wooing of a sort of Christ-like integrity that draws us more into the presence and the being of God and encourages us to take others on that journey, too (Ireland);

✧ [that] you have to be God-like. You have to be Christ-like, and that is holiness for me (Pakistan);

✧ mostly associated with not being corrupt (India/Germany);

- ✧ a heavenly trait that has embraced our land since our risen Lord has imprinted his footsteps on its soil ... a piece of heaven here on earth; we call it 'Lebanon', the Land of Holiness (Lebanon);

- ✧ [that,] during the last few years, we've had five grand-children, and I describe holiness as holding our first new-born grandchild and then every other grandchild for the very first time and realizing that's exactly how our heav-enly Father sees us every single day (United Kingdom);

- ✧ to live following the teachings of God (Argentina);

- ✧ living a life of integrity, living a life that is pleasing to God (India);

- ✧ the process of growing into the image of Christ (Palestine);

- ✧ being set apart for God (Pakistan);

- ✧ me not adding other zeros behind [a] figure, even if the budgets can accommodate it (Nigeria);

- ✧ just trying to walk with Christ (Sri Lanka);

- ✧ something that I am aspiring to (Canada);

- ✧ a kind of being one with what you say (South Sudan);

- ✧ spelled out in a concern, an active concern, for those who cannot care for themselves, for the desperately needy, the marginalized and the helpless (United States);

- ✧ this feeling almost, this drive to become, this understand-ing that there's more to you in life, and this feeling that pushes you to want to do more, wanting to be better, wanting to become a better version of yourself, continu-ally (Trinidad);

- ✧ living by example, being considerate to others and their needs and being a light in darkness radiating the light of Christ. And to me it is a privilege of living as a people, set aside or set apart, and longing for the power of the Holy

> Spirit to work within me to produce a godly character and
> conduct (South Sudan/United Kingdom);
>
> ✧ having a personal relationship with God and that relation-
> ship extending to our fellow human beings, respecting the
> rights of individuals, respecting individual beings, look-
> ing at individuals as people created in the image of God
> (Ghana);
>
> ✧ taking risks, so all people are loved and treated fairly.
> That's holiness (Guyana);
>
> ✧ not just being stuck in our cathedrals and saying elaborate
> prayers, but be[ing] on the ground active, challenging those
> unjust structures of society, as an act of holiness. I think
> my biggest challenge is that [when] you try to challenge
> some of these systems and structures, the perpetrators,
> those in authority, those in power, always descend on you
> and ensure that you are muzzled somehow, so that you do
> not exercise your ministry as you should (Zimbabwe).

Our Call to 'Holiness' and Our Identity in Christ

Holiness is connected across our world and in 1 Peter 2 both
to God and to action. Holiness across Scripture, from Leviticus
to 1 Peter, is all about how we relate to one another and to
God. Holiness is always interdependent. What 1 Peter adds to
holiness is that it cannot be detached from Christ. In this way,
holiness is not simply an abstention from the bad, but an imitation of God in God's self-sacrificial movement towards the
other, which is most explicit in Jesus Christ.

Holiness is about the transformation of all that is not holy
into something that is good. Imitating God's movement towards
us should determine the action, discipline and behaviour – or,
we could say, the ethics – within the Christian community.
Holiness is not about performative piety, nor is it something

that we can earn: it is the gift of the grace of God, given by God and God alone. Holiness is the very movement of God, and it leads to transformation. We do not have to have certain abilities to be holy: the marginalized, the weak, the poor, the disabled, the elderly and children can all be holy. When we look at this theme of holiness – holy life, holy sacrifice, holy people-hood – across 1 Peter, we can explain it all in terms of a single and marvellous act of God: that he calls us out of darkness into light, turning nobodies into a nation and bestowing divine forgiveness on the unforgiven.

The entire act of God described here constitutes the life, passion, death and resurrection of Jesus, the self-giving of God for sinful human beings, that takes them with him to his own glory. Holiness is supremely manifest in God coming close to the unholy and thereby transforming unholiness into all that is holy through God's own character of self-sacrificing love. This is a central Gospel proclamation: 'But God proves his love for us in that, while we were still sinners, Christ died for us' (Rom. 5.8), and this proclamation is given a form within human life and relationship: 'Love your enemies' (Matt. 5.44; Luke 6.27, 35).

Holiness in 1 Peter has a profound centre in Christ, since it describes the act of God in Christ moving towards what is unholy in order to transform it. 'Stones' become 'living'; those who were 'not a people' become God's people; those who are 'scattered', 'strangers' and 'lost' are gathered together 'in Christ'. As Christians are joined to Christ, they share in Christ's divine character; and as they love with Christ, they display and receive his gifts. The church's holiness is one oriented to others, not only to the holy within the church, but to the unholy as well, both within and outside the church. This was clear in the earlier reflections in the excursus on holiness: holiness is drawing close to the marginalized and moving closer to God. Nevertheless, the call to demonstrate holy living through walking with Christ is difficult. Many relentless pressures, both internal and external, are brought to bear against our desire to live holy lives. Let us return to our conversation with three brothers and sisters in Christ to learn about their understanding of holiness from their different contexts.

Discussion Part Two: Holiness and Hospitality

Each bishop engages with the prompt: When did you discover the value and importance of holiness in your own personal or ministry journey? How is it that we understand 'holy' in our contexts?

Bishop Manuel says that holiness is not tolerance, nor is it being driven by what one individual may think is right and wrong. Holiness, rather, is a sacred space that is embodied in us, the life of the Holy Trinity. Holiness is a response to God's great love for us. Holiness is a gift that comes from God, it is a call that comes from God and it is a rediscovery of our purpose. We were spared, we were chosen, for a certain purpose. That purpose is to dedicate ourselves to serving God, to dedicate ourselves to the service of the other, and this is especially important in new faith areas and in areas where we have to live with brothers and sisters from other faith families. It is very important that we have and radiate these values of God and that people are inspired by our example, so they may be drawn closer to Christ and to one another. It is because they can see there is something greater than us here that they see a community being formed and desire to belong to it. That's why the church is growing.

Bishop Stephen agrees that holiness is a gift from God. Especially in his context in which the surrounding majority are Muslim, but in which they want to plant churches, focus on discipleship and build leaders. Holiness is the gift of love from God, and our response to that is holiness. Bishop Stephen offers an example, that of anti-corruption.

Anti-corruption is very important in Christian ethics and understanding, as corruption is not holy. Therefore, we take a firm stand against it. In Malaysia, however, there are decrees (fatwas) saying that corruption is actually a gift (from God), and that there is nothing wrong with it. He asks: 'How do we continue to be holy in a way we are not offensive or just merely tolerated, but to be respected?' The answer lies in another question: 'Are we only being selective in our holiness and expression of holiness? Is it only in terms of corruption [that] we want to raise the banner, but in other ways we don't walk the talk?' For Bishop Stephen and his diocese, dealing with the various surrounding faiths, people come to them and want to know whether God is with them, whether the holiness is embodied in their community or not. Being holy can sometimes mean making other people uncomfortable.

Bishop Phoebe speaks of holiness in her context, in the southern United States, where there is great political division, and where many keep in their inner circles only those who look like them. Our inner circles are not made up of a diversity of races and ethnicities, and so the church is really grappling with what it means to reflect the fullness of the communities in which we are located. This reminds Bishop Phoebe of the call to hospitality and of the ways in which God demonstrates hospitality. For God, there is room for everyone at the table. We should thus ask ourselves who is missing from our table: 'Who is in my inner circle? Whose voices are a part of my decision-making process?' When we ask ourselves who is missing, then we begin to cross barriers. And when we cross barriers and reach out to people who haven't always been included, who haven't always had a voice, then we can find ourselves uncomfortable, but we try to enter into this work with a great spirit of humility. As you are reaching out and embracing, there is so much learning on all sides. It is a grace from God that enables us to do this, but there's something about relationship-building, providing hospitality and really seeing God in other people that is an integral part, for Bishop Phoebe, of what it means to try to be a holy people.

Bishop Manuel agrees that hospitality is a matter of opening doors to one another and the wider community, but he recognizes the profound implications this can have. Human beings generally want to preserve themselves and generally want to preserve holiness for themselves. But Bishop Manuel thinks holiness and hospitality are spiritual disciplines. Only with spirituality, he says, can we understand this dimension, this invitation from God. Bishop Stephen, reflecting on his fellow bishops' thoughts, says it has dawned on him that 'hospitality equals holy space'.

Further Exposition of 1 Peter 2

As Bishop Stephen has just reflected, 'hospitality equals holy space'. But why in and throughout Scripture are we meant to be hospitable? We are meant to be hospitable because the ancient Israelites were exiled strangers and aliens. Holy living therefore means hospitality: it means welcoming the stranger and the alien. Holiness means caring for the other, seeing the other as they are and welcoming those in our communities even if they are not the same as us. Holiness is not just toleration, and we have seen that sometimes, in Christian history, people weaponized holiness.

We must acknowledge that there is a massive power dynamic attached to holiness, especially when we think we know who is holy and who is not. While agency is given to those who are deemed 'holy' – bishops, archbishops and other leaders in the church – to exclude that which is not holy, such a view raises questions about their concomitant agency to include or exclude. We must remember that what makes one holy and thus included is not wholly human action, but divine grace and human response.

We find Moses saying in Deuteronomy to the Israelites, ['F]or you are a people holy to the Lord your God; it is you the Lord has chosen out of all the peoples on earth to be his people, his treasured possession' (14.2). In other words, the boundary between inclusion and exclusion is set by God. If only God can determine what is holy and who is holy, then, what does this mean for us, as Christians, for the ways in which we exclude and include? What does it mean for us as a church when we separate ourselves from one another because we have decided who is and who is not holy? How often do we make holy our way of being by claiming it for the divine, and using it to exclude others, for whatever reason, because we fear them – because of their gender, because of their race, because of their sexuality or because of their marital status?

The language of holiness, depending on the theology one holds in terms of God's actions and ours, encourages extreme stances, of both inclusion and exclusion. We only need to think of Acts 10, where it took a vision from God to convince Peter that 'what God has made clean, you must not call profane' (10.15), and that this had to happen three times before Peter was convinced that that which he had excluded was no longer excluded by God. 1 Peter never says that holiness means that one must separate oneself from that which is not holy. When we do that, all too often we conflate and confuse holiness with purity, and these are not the same thing. And yet, there are places in our world where holiness is purity and where, for example, single mothers are not holy, singleness is not holy, people of different sexual identities are not holy. Peter (and Leviticus, on which he relies) is clear that holiness is not something over which we have any power or control; holiness is the very movement of God, and Jesus is the only one who can make the unholy holy.

Holiness is the movement of God. We might separate ourselves because we have judged ourselves or another to be
unholy, but the call of the Christian is to live on the border of
the holy, just as Jesus himself loved and broke bread with those
considered 'unholy' in his own time. Holiness is hospitality; it is
love of the other. Christ even became sin for us, dying an unholy
death as a criminal on a cross, in order to draw the whole world
to himself. The call to holiness is always derivative, grounded
in Christ. A person is holy, the church is holy, a community
is holy, only because Christ is in the midst of it. Peter returns
to Christ as the one who is holy and as the one who makes us
holy. Holiness, therefore, is not about *us*: it is about the actions
of God and the identity we are given by God. Holiness doesn't
ask everyone to look and think alike, but it does ask all to put
aside malice and to embrace the call to mutual love. We are,
however, responsible for discipline, a space where holiness can
grow, and for guidance of others to God, who is holy. We also
have to remember that 1 Peter addresses communities, not individuals. And, within these communities, there are people who
urge us not to personal discipline and personal holiness but to
unity and community, to offer a living hope, to transformation
and inclusion.

The shepherd is called to be holy, which means fighting the
lion, not the sheep. Multifarious identities – so many areas
and backgrounds – are at work in the church. This is a hugely
important point – not because we want everyone to look alike,
but because we want to put aside malice and love one another.
Holiness and identity (and vocation) revolve here around the
declaration: 'In order that you may proclaim the mighty acts
of [God]' (1 Pet. 2.9). Being inward-looking or circling the
wagons is not holiness. Jesus's incarnation, life, death, resurrection and ascension and the sending of the Holy Spirit into an
unholy world show that separation is not the same as holiness.
How do we walk together with those who are alien and exiled?
What would it look like to love everyone as a chosen person
of God? What do we do when we separate ourselves from the
other because we have decided that the other is *not* holy? What

are we doing to ourselves and to them? To help us engage with these questions, we return one final time to the wisdom and experience of Bishops Phoebe, Manuel and Stephen.

Discussion Part Three: Holiness and Hospitality

This panel discussion goes to a number of places: one is about walking apart and that walking together doesn't mean 'here I stand and I move no further', but that walking apart is like the parables of the lost. Holiness is celebrating when the lost return. In reality, we aren't ever fully separated. How can we listen to one another and stand in our own truths and understand that we are all from different places? This is not about everybody agreeing but allowing us each to stand in our truths and for there still to be mutual love and affection for one another. We have to show, in our politics and in how we live together, that we are walking in a way of love, of charity, and not of arrogance. We can only do this when we remember that God is with us and that we are not alone, literally or figuratively. There is a great danger that we are driven to ways that are not holy. What is driving our reflections together in the church? How can we progress together? What is our faith, our history and our legacy together? We have so much to learn from one another, and if God really is on the side of the marginalized and overlooked, then we have much more work to do. How can we listen and learn from one another?

Bishop Stephen speaks of hospitality and holiness as meaning the necessity, sometimes, of walking apart or of waiting with arms wide open like the father in the story of the 'Prodigal Son' waiting for his lost sons, both the one at home and the one that left only to return. It is significant that the father waits; we cannot force these moments. Difficult as it may be, we must allow space for another person to come back. The son at home, who thought that he was always there and not lost, must also realize he actually is lost, come to his senses and return. Celebrating such returns is holiness. This is not to say that we all must have the same understanding of holiness, but that this walking about and walking together does not mean 'here I stand and I move no further'; this is not the sense of holiness and hospitality that we get from the parables of the lost coin, sheep and son.

Bishop Phoebe mentions the question of formation: 'Do we know whose we are, who is holding us as we enter into this work?' It strikes Bishop Phoebe that community is very important. Being a Christian is not a vocation for a lone ranger, and neither is being a bishop and leader in the church. There is great diversity within the worldwide church. Bishop Phoebe expresses concerns she felt before participating at the Lambeth Conference due to her being a woman from the American context. She wondered how she would be received by all her brothers and sisters in Christ. This anxiety reminded her of the necessity of her own practice of prayer and grounding in Scripture, as well as the necessity of trying to enter into these spaces not assuming the worst, but giving people the benefit of the doubt. Although this can be difficult, particularly because, as she acknowledges, she would probably hear things that challenged her worldview, she knows she can choose how to respond. 'Am I going to become defensive or shut people down, or can I stand in my own truth, my own embodied right reality as a woman of colour from the American context and understand that other people are at different places?' At the end of the day, she says, it isn't about everybody agreeing in some sort of superficial, surface-level way, but about how we can stand in our truths and allow others to stand in their truths and yet still demonstrate mutual love and affection for one another.

Bishop Manuel speaks of how important it is, in a politically, religiously and socially plural context, to show who we are and whom we follow: Jesus Christ. We must be confident in who we are and whom we follow, but we must also demonstrate this confidence in a loving way, in a charitable way, so that we don't appear arrogant. Our relationships with ourselves, with our brothers and sisters and with those from other communities, will show others who we are. In this way we can move forward together and bring about the return of our common faith. Bishop Manuel is especially looking forward to knowing whether we can transform our conversations, such as has been happening at this Lambeth Conference, and whether fellow Christians can and will take this rediscovery of spiritual disciplines like holiness, humility and hospitality to their communities and societies.

Bishop Phoebe concludes: 'I'm just so convicted by the fact that God sees the people that I don't see, and God loves the people that I don't love. And if I'm allowing myself to be transformed – if my [community] is open to transformation – then we too will begin to see and love things that we don't right now.' God invites us, she says, to let in the light, make space for more people and extend our boundaries. She is 'really excited about learning, from my brother and sister bishops, the ways in which they have been open to God's transforming and healing and reconciling love in their own contexts ... What can I bring back to West Tennessee?'

Conclusion

How we live as God's holy people affects how we live together and impacts all our relationships. We have engaged with three articulations of a deep desire to learn, to listen, to embrace and to evangelize, all as a part of moving towards God and one another in our call to mutual love and holiness. Bishops Stephen, Phoebe and Manuel have shared both their desire to listen and learn, and their anxiety that they will not be heard. Christ starts not where we should be, but with the church. Even so, God comes to us where we are, and when he comes to us, we are called to repentance and change. But we are a church that no longer shakes hands and shares the peace or a common table. What does this mean for unity in Christ, for reconciliation and for relationship with brothers and sisters in Christ?

We may be divided by so many things, but how do we come together and understand ourselves and our church as God's holy people, as one in Christ? How do we listen to each other's stories? Reconciliation with brothers and sisters in Christ means that we have to be able to listen to another person's story and repeat it back to them in such a way that they recognize it as *their* story. We might not agree, but we need to understand.

Questions for Bible Study

Living Stones: 1 Peter 2.1, 11: 'Rid yourselves, therefore, of all malice, and all guile, insincerity, envy, and all slander ... Beloved, I urge you as aliens and exiles to abstain from the desires of the flesh that wage war against the soul.'

The terms used in 2.1 – malice (evil), guile (deception), insincerity, envy and slander – can be a little difficult to understand. While these vices are clearly present in the world today, we have to think carefully in order to identify when we feel envy or malice or when we are acting with guile, insincerity or slander. Reflect personally on the list of vices in 1 Peter 2: in your own

---

life, do you see (or have you seen) malice, guile, insincerity, envy, or slander?

In your community or nation, what are one or two 'desires of the flesh' that need to be confronted by the church? Keep in mind the differences within communities and cultures about what 'desires of the flesh' might need to be confronted.

Honourable Conduct: 1 Peter 2.12: 'Conduct yourselves honourably among the Gentiles, so that, though they malign you as evildoers, they may see your honourable deeds and glorify God when he comes to judge.'

Reflect on the following questions:
✧ Think about your own church or community. What sort of honourable conduct in your context would be so compelling and powerful that it would cause unbelievers to glorify God?
✧ What sort of conduct in your context would be so compelling that it would lead to praise of the church by non-Christian leaders?

Suffering for doing what is right: 1 Peter 2.20–21: 'But if you endure when you do right and suffer for it, you have God's approval. For to this you have been called, because Christ also suffered for you, leaving you an example, so that you should follow in his steps.'

Reflect on situations of injustice in your life, country or community. In these situations, how have you or your church been complicit in suffering or not acted in places where a difference could have been made? What might you change?

What might it mean to repent for past failings?

3

Resistance and Resilience in Christ

1 Peter 2.13 — 3.22

The words of 1 Peter 2.13—3.22 have been used to justify great evil. They have been used to support slavery, to uphold empire and to defend those who perpetrate domestic violence. We know in our hearts that slavery, domestic violence and empire building are wrong. This is our instinctive response. But we also have to recognize that we are part of a church that – whether we like it or not – has a history wrapped up in empire, power-seeking, subjugation and furthering it. We have a history of both resistance as well as complicity with these systems.

Invitations to the First Lambeth Conference and to Conversation

In 1867, Archbishop Longley invited bishops to the first Lambeth Conference. It was a chance to 'discuss the peculiar difficulties and perplexities in which our widely-scattered Colonial Churches [were] involved, and the evils to which they [were] exposed'. These churches were bound together 'only by the ties of kindred ... to offer up united prayers and praise to the Most High in the mother tongue common to us all ...' Thus, Archbishop Longley's invitation to the first Lambeth Conference reads as follows:

Right Revd and Dear Brother, I request your presence at a meeting of the bishops in visible communion with the United Church of England and Ireland, proposed (God willing) to be holden at Lambeth, under my presidency, on the 24th of September next and the three following days ... I [have been] moved to invite the bishops of our Indian and Colonial Episcopate to meet myself and the Home bishops for brother-ly communion and conference ... [and] all who are avowedly in communion with our Church. (Stephenson 1978, p. 32)

Here is an excerpt from the Archbishop's Opening Address at this first Lambeth Conference in 1867:

Many have been the anxious thought and great the heart-searchings which have attended the preparations for this remarkable manifestation of life and energy in the several branches of our communion. The origin of this Conference has already been stated in the circular of invitation which I addressed to you all. It was at the instance of the Metropoli-tan and Bishops of the Church of Canada, supported by the unanimous request of a very large meeting of Archbishops and Bishops of the Home and Colonial Church ... We rejoice to find that so many of our brethren from distant parts of the globe have been moved to respond to the call, and we welcome with feelings of cordial affection and genuine sympathy the presence of so large a proportion of the American Episcopate. From very many also, who, owing to various circumstances, have been prevented from joining us, I have received letters expressing the profound satisfaction and thankfulness with which they regard the opportunities afforded by this gather-ing for conferring together upon topics of mutual interest, *for discussing the peculiar difficulties and perplexities in which our widely-scattered Colonial Churches are involved, and the evils to which they are exposed*; for cementing yet more firmly the bonds of Christian communion between Churches, acknowledging one Lord, one faith, one baptism – *connected not only by the ties of kindred, but ... to offer up united prayers and praise to the Most High in the mother tongue common to us all ...* (Project Canterbury, italics added)

We are now going to reflect and think for a moment on these foundational words for that first Lambeth Conference. The invitation and opening address are given to 'our widely scattered Colonial Churches' who are bound together not only by Christian faith but also 'by the ties of kindred' and a 'mother tongue', and all in union with 'the Mother-Church'. We will do this firstly by engaging three questions:

• What do these words from Archbishop Longley say to you?
• Are they shocking? Why?
• How have we, as a church, collaborated with empire, or colluded with empire and structural sin (such as slavery, abuse and the condemnation of brothers and sisters in Christ)?

Exposition of 1 Peter 2.13 – 3.22

The uncomfortable truth is that the church has power. We are the institution and the empire. Every church leader, lay or ordained, is connected with institution and thus has power and authority in some way – perhaps by virtue of our office, our position, our connection with the church, our gender or our socio-economic class – even if not in other ways. We say that empire is unacceptable, but we are also complicit on account of the ways we relate to one another.

What do we see when we look at ourselves? What happens when we make visible the structures of empire and the history and present reality of power? And what do we do with the reality that accepting structures of power, empire, slavery and submission of women are part of our Scripture? We are good at condemning some of these things, but we certainly don't do so uniformly. For example, wives and slaves are explicitly compared in 1 Peter, and yet we are often more confident in condemning slavery than we are in condemning systems that keep women, girls and wives in situations of domestic violence, abuse and exploitation. In many parts of the contemporary world, including many parts of the global church, such a distinction that involves condemning slavery but not the abuse and exploitation of women is made and practised.

The system of slavery – a system that must be rejected in contemporary contexts by Christians – is seen as part of the ancient world. The system of patriarchy is, however, maintained by many Christians who align contemporary socio-cultural norms with ancient socio-cultural norms and thereby sanctify them. 1 Peter does not allow us to make this distinction. Let us now look carefully at this text together.

For many in our global church, 1 Peter is a difficult letter. Faced with a text that appears to accept the authority of human institutions, slavery, and submission of wives or women, we are challenged by how best to interpret this text, and even more to know how best to live it out and be faithful to the lesson it teaches us. What are we to do with a text of this sort? First, Peter takes up the topic of submission to the government. In 1 Peter 2.13–17, Peter instructs his hearers to be subject to all human institutions, especially the 'emperors' or 'governors sent by him'. How we understand the command to 'accept the authority of' depends largely on how we understand the phrase 'for the Lord's sake' at the start, which motivates such action.

It is worth pondering the possibility that 1 Peter may be offering a deliberately ambiguous command. We could read these verses as an argument for the authority of the emperor and his governors as part of God's order – that is, God has sent them. Or, we could read these verses as an argument for the emperor and his governors as (a mere) part of the dominant human order – that is, the emperor has established them. The difference is significant, and it is worth noting that such ambiguity is a characteristic of literature aimed at those who are marginalized, outsiders and aliens. Were those of the dominant order – the emperor or his governors – to intercept such literature, they would understand the text in one way, while the intended recipients would hear something quite different.

This section advocates a strategic submission to the order of the empire, but also an ultimate, essential submission to God. Even so, this primary submission cannot be used as an excuse for evil. There are many lordless powers in our world today whose authority seems so pervasive that we often fail to question our existence within them and our relationship to them. We are often called to 'accept the authority of' these powers, even when we would prefer – or feel called – to resist their various facets: financial systems and the source of some of our investments; international trading; systems that exploit the vulnerable, the refugee, the child and the sex worker; or systems that tolerate domestic violence and encourage human trafficking. What Peter does for us is make visible the invisible structures of our world, and in particular the insidious mechanisms of empire: human institution, slavery and submission.

This section of 1 Peter 2 climaxes with some key reminders to Peter's recipients, making clear what their priorities and distinctions should be. While those in the community should honour everyone, including the emperor, they should only fear God and love the community of believers. 'Honour' as an outward virtue is appropriate for all, including the emperor; 'love' as an inner virtue is required for the community of believers; and 'fear' (or awe) is the appropriate stance toward God. For Peter, in contrast to the honour that is due to all, 'fear/reverence is reserved for God alone and [in this letter, fear] is more prominent as a motivation for exhortation than in any New Testament writing' (Elliott 2000, p. 500, citing Goppelt, p. 190). The letter then turns to two dominant systems of human institutions, slavery and patriarchy, which are the two most prevalent and enduring systems of the ancient world, so widespread that they are all but invisible. *Remarkably, just like structures of empire, this letter makes them visible.*

It is worth noting that this letter addresses slaves and wives directly. They are the subjects of these sections. They are seen, recognized and acknowledged as human beings with their own inner lives. We must recognize with Peter just how precarious life is for the slaves who are part of the community of believers. Because they serve two masters – the slave-master and God – there is a dangerous tension at the very core of their lives. Because they are members of 'God's chosen people' and members of the system of slavery, they live with the unbearable reality of freedom, both free in Christ and slaves in the Graeco-Roman system, God's chosen and liberated people, yet shackled and with little choice themselves. Still, Scripture offers multiple ways to respond to such tensions, ranging from overt resistance to the dominant system (as in Ex. 3) to conformity with it (as in Rom. 13). In the exhortation to the slaves within his community of faith, Peter errs on the side of survival. Resistance to powerful and deep-rooted systems such as slavery could well lead to death. Peter holds in tension faithfulness and survival.

These exhortations to honour the emperor while fearing God and that Christian slaves not respond in sin when treated unjustly demonstrate to us the vulnerability of most Christians in the first century. These Christians were on the margins, confirming for us what Peter means when he calls his community 'aliens and exiles'. 1 Peter encourages Christians today who find themselves in positions of persecution and marginalization and reminds Christians living in predominantly Christian societies to not grow too comfortable or be lulled into complacency.

We cannot neglect being aware of how easily one could become vulnerable to systems of power within the ancient world and still can in our world today. The theological line 1 Peter takes in encouraging resilience is to align the unjust suffering of the persecuted – those who are doing right – with the unjust suffering of Christ himself. Peter clarifies that Christ's suffering is not merely a historical fact, but is an example for the listeners and readers of the letter who are to 'follow in his steps' (2.21). Thus, Jesus not only left his followers an example, teaching them to endure suffering in a God-honouring fashion, but he also, by freeing them from the power of sin, offered them a model for living, enabling them to endure suffering and live justly in the midst of injustice. Christ's example of resilient endurance in the face of systemic, unjust suffering is an actual, lived reality.

Peter concludes this section with the image of the shepherd and the sheep. He reminds his community that they were once straying sheep who had been brought back by the shepherd who laid down his life for his sheep and was now the 'guardian of [their] souls' (2.25). Even as they endure suffering, they are being watched over, contended for, by the shepherd who knew full well what it was to endure injustice and who would indeed ultimately vindicate their suffering, just as the Father had vindicated him. The image of the shepherd will return to the forefront of Peter's exhortation and his understanding of Christ in chapter 5.

The letter then turns away from slaves to wives. This new section begins with 'in the same way' (1 Pet. 3.1), which directly connects these two forms of authority and prompts us to grapple theologically with a text from Scripture that uses the same kind of argument for slaves and women or wives. In the ancient world, slaves and women occupied a similar social status as objects of elite men. Neither slaves nor women had power, situating them well in the wider community of aliens and exiles in 1 Peter, since we must remember that aliens and exiles do not have power either.

The repetition of the phrase 'accept the authority of their/your husbands' recognizes the constraints of the ancient world on women. Women belonged to their husbands. Peter recognizes this cultural reality, but seems to subvert it as well. Peter is clear that these women are not to be ordered or intimidated by their husbands, but rather they are to 'do what is good' in the sight of God and 'never let fears alarm [them]' (3.6). We may note that, once again, Peter counsels survival: 'doing what is good' within the system in order to survive the system. This is also a call that summons the believer to trust that, by ordering their lives in God's sight, they will survive and will even have the opportunity to witness and give an account for the hope that is in them.

The letter then turns to 'husbands'. The repetition of 'in the same way' suggests that there is, once again, a similar argument here (3.7). Husbands are exhorted to recognize that women generally – and their own wives in particular – are the 'weaker sex' (literally: 'vulnerable bodies') in this alien world, and so to 'pay honour' to their wives who are 'also heirs of the gracious gift of life' in God (3.7). They must do what the dominant order does not do: honour those whom society considers beneath it and thus also subvert the system. Peter then ends with a warning to 'husbands'. If they do not follow this godly way of life, but instead conform to the way of life of the dominant powers, they face the danger of disruption in their relationship with God and the risk that their 'prayers' 'may [be] hinder[ed]'. For 1 Peter, a right relationship with God requires a right relationship with women.

There are parts of our contemporary world where little has changed from Peter's time. There are parts of our world in which the system of slavery has been rejected by the Church, but not the system of patriarchy. And there are parts of our world in which both systems have been rejected. Such different contexts will mean we all approach 1 Peter quite differently. But Peter then turns to 'all' (3.8). He is not just addressing a select group who are supposed to be unified, but everyone. All are called to unity and sympathy together; reconciliation requires compassion, sympathy, suffering, humility and love. While Peter, up to this point, has dealt with different parts of the community in turn, giving different wisdom for slaves, wives and husbands, Peter now asserts that the 'unity' of the community is vital. The conclusion to this section mirrors the start: they are, together in Christ, a holy people, a chosen nation. There is a single calling, even if its application may differ depending on their individual circumstances. By 'sanctify[ing] Christ as Lord' in their hearts, they will have opportunities to give 'an account of the hope' that resides in them (3.15).

The question Peter continues to grapple with in this section is this: how do those who are required 'to accept the authority of' the dominant systems of the day – slavery and patriarchy

– reconcile this submission with the call to 'sanctify Christ as Lord' (3.15)? 1 Peter 3.15–16 serves as a hinge for the whole of the letter, as those who follow Christ are told to be ready to testify to the hope that is in them, even in the midst of great suffering. This is not dreary work, but a testimony of joy in the resurrected victory of Christ, who offers a living hope and to whom in the end all powers submit. Jesus is always victor, so that those who live under conditions they cannot control – illness, pain, displacement, unjust regimes, unjust authority – all live as children of this Lord who was, in his suffering, redeeming the world and who is, in his victory, Lord and judge of this world. The central affirmation in this chapter, as in the letter as a whole, is that we are not left comfortless. We live in a world where Christ is Lord.

So, while it may look to us – in the midst of what are some-times difficult and even unbearable situations for us – that others are in control of this world, there is, by virtue of the resurrection of Christ, only one true judge and Lord and we are both the 'living stones' of his house and his own holy people. So, how do we give an account of the hope that is in us, espe-cially when our world is suffering from a deficit of gentleness, kindness and hope? How do we challenge systems of power but also dismantle fear, especially when such power threatens death for Christians across our globe, and when the fear is very real indeed? These questions will help as we start thinking about power, power imbalances and increasing awareness of and the ability to name power differentials and our own individual positions of power, whatever they may be.

If we cannot recognize where we have power, we can become dangerous. Christians who take their own power seriously are more conscious of their vulnerability. When we recognize whatever power we may have, such power can be responsibly tempered and used to empower others, rather than abused for personal or institutional gain. How do we recognize power and what power we have in a situation?

We rarely seem to think that we are strong or that we have power. As we talk about issues of power, we have to recognize that power can look different in different relationships and from different perspectives. Despite the 'strength' of money, comfort and medicine, someone in Canada, the United States or the United Kingdom might feel weaker because the Global North is outnumbered by the Global South. On the other hand, a Christian in Pakistan, Nigeria or Ghana might feel vulnerable because they are a persecuted minority – but in different contexts they are mighty indeed. Different identities that can lead to a sense of power or powerlessness come to the fore in different contexts. We also have to remember and address the power that Christian leaders have internally. In many parts of our global church, the leader's word is final and cannot be questioned. Any exercise of power that denies it is an exercise of power is dangerous. Power that is recognized can, however, be used to empower others. Power can be shared – and not necessarily at one's own cost – resulting in a better situation for all; power is not a zero-sum game. The more it is shared, the more there is, and the more it can be used for the benefit of others.

The invitation to the first Lambeth Conference was laden with words of empire, patriarchy and colonialism, but it was also a call to come together to pray, to be united with one another and to hold on to hope. This call is found in 1 Peter: the call to unity, to follow in Christ's footsteps, to keep hold of hope that is held for us in Christ and to practise genuine, constant, mutual love for all those in Jesus Christ. Genuine mutual love is the greatest way to subvert abuse of power, and all of us, not just a few, are called to give an account of hope.

How, like Peter, do we move from singling out sectors and groups in our global church to understanding that Christ exhorts 'all' to give an account of the hope we find in him? All of those addressed, especially enslaved persons, those under empire and women, are chosen by God. They are a holy nation and God's holy, chosen people.

As Professor Kate Sonderegger reflected, 1 Peter is fully realistic about what it is like to live in a world that we don't control but that nonetheless shapes us.[1] Such a reality is just as true in our friendships and marriages as it is true in our work lives and existence as citizens of a particular nation. Peter asks us to consider how we might live under structures and people that we cannot control or shape, and yet reflect on how we can, under those conditions, return blessing, testify to hope and remain faithful to Christ.

Questions for Bible Study

Empire: 1 Peter 2.17: 'Honour everyone, Love the family of believers. Fear God. Honour the emperor.'

Reflect on the following questions:
✧ How do these commands from 1 Peter speak to you and your situation?
✧ Are any of these commands harder to follow than others?

Authority: 1 Peter connects submission to human institutions (such as empire and the emperor) both with the submission of slaves to masters and the submission of wives to husbands, with a focus on unbelieving husbands.

1 Peter 2.13: 'For the Lord's sake accept the authority of every human institution ...'; 1 Peter 2.18: 'Slaves, accept the authority of your masters with all deference ...'; 1 Peter 3.1: 'Wives, in the same way, accept the authority of your husbands ...'; 1 Peter 3.8–9: 'Finally, all of you, have unity of spirit, sympathy, love for one another, a tender heart, and a humble mind. Do not repay evil for evil or abuse for abuse; but, on the contrary, repay with a blessing.'

---

1 See the Lambeth Conference Video on 1 Peter 3 by Professor Kate Sonderegger: https://www.lambethconference.org/phase-1/watch-the-1-peter-videos/ (accessed 7.9.23).

Reflect on the following questions:
✧ Think for a moment about a situation where you feel power-less or persecuted because of your faith. What image does this situation bring to mind?
✧ What would it mean to resist that situation and what would it mean to endure that situation?
✧ How do you know when you should bear up under insult and evil and when you should defend yourself?
✧ Is it possible for you to give a blessing instead of returning evil or insult to those who are harsh, punishing or silencing towards you? Why or why not?
✧ How might we support all who live under systems of oppression and all who live under the authority of harsh, unjust or silencing powers?

Hope: 1 Peter 3.15–16: 'Always be ready to make your defence to anyone who demands from you an account of the hope that is in you; yet do it with gentleness and reverence.'

Reflect on the following questions:
✧ What does it mean to live in a way that makes other people ask you about the source of your hope?
✧ What would you say to someone who asked you to give an account of your hope?

References

Elliott, John H., 2000, *1 Peter: A New Translation with Introduction and Commentary*, Anchor Bible Commentary Series 37.2 (New York: Doubleday).

Project Canterbury, 'Conference of Bishops of the Anglican Communion, Holden at Lambeth Palace, September 24–27, 1867', http://anglicanhistory.org/lambeth/conference_bishops1867.html (accessed 7.9.23).

Stephenson, Alan M. G., 1978, *Anglicanism and the Lambeth Conferences* (London: SPCK).

4

Suffering in Christ

1 Peter 4

Introduction

Suffering is mentioned more times in 1 Peter than in any other New Testament text, but Peter is not writing about just any suffering. He is writing about the suffering of Jesus Christ and suffering in Christ's name. For Peter, suffering is a condition of being a Christian. We have faith in the redemptive suffering of Jesus Christ, but, because of this, we have a tendency to make *all* suffering redemptive. Peter challenges this temptation, because when we equate *all* suffering with Christ, we can advocate staying in abusive situations. Suffering can become an excuse to not do anything about injustice or wrong. People told to bear abuse to be saved brings us right back to the reflection on 1 Peter 2–3 about power and how easy it is to be complicit ourselves.

1 Peter was written to a small group of Christians, a minority in their culture, who lived in a hostile empire that was fearful of their beliefs and viewed them with suspicion. Within this context, Peter is speaking only about suffering for the name of Christ. Peter is pointing to persecution for one's faith. In some parts of our world, that persecution might take the form of being mocked or ridiculed. But in other places, this persecution involves the daily threat of physical violence, oppression and even death. We should not be too quick to claim the language of persecution before we listen to and acknowledge the depth

and reality of suffering for the name of Christ in our world. We must also be aware of how suffering is understood in different ways across our communities and contexts, which we find in the testimonies within the following excursus.

Excursus: Voices on Suffering

In my context, suffering is:

✧ our daily bread and the air that we breathe since forever (Lebanon);

✧ quite commonplace in Sri Lanka right now (Sri Lanka);

✧ very much a tangible reality in the Palestinian context (Palestine);

✧ the mother who breastfeeds her baby after going for days without a meal, the mother who goes without [so] that her children might have – that's suffering (Guyana);

✧ when I see the refugees in my country living in concentration camps (Uganda);

✧ [that] there is nothing as painful as leading a divided church (Zimbabwe);

✧ a struggle with mental health and having the courage to open up and ask others for help when needed (Canada);

✧ if I have had any sense of suffering in my calling, [that] there is sometimes a cost in maintaining a vision of spaciousness within the body of Christ and even within Anglicanism (Ireland);

✧ [that] I've personally suffered pain in my family. I lost loved ones and that has really caused me a lot of pain and anguish. I've also experienced suffering because of displacement and refugee life that many of us in South Sudan would identify with (South Sudan/United Kingdom);

✧ in the work that I do with those seeking asylum and those seeking refuge, suffering is waiting for others to make decisions about their future. Suffering is the sense of having [one's] life put on hold, and it's the gradual erosion of hope (Cyprus);

✧ when people find no hope, when people find no reason and purpose to continue to witness in the land where it all started – we're talking about the Holy Land. Suffering means that you don't find yourself, and [that] you're disconnected with your history, with your culture and with your future (Israel);

✧ in northern Nigeria, when Christians are persecuted for their faith. They are deliberately left out; their areas, their locations, are not being looked after by the government today because they are Christians (Nigeria);

✧ the heart of the Christian gospel. Recently in [the] northern and southern parts of India, many pastors, evangelists, missionaries [and] nuns were raped and murdered for the proclamation of good news to the poor people (India);

✧ [that] food prices have really gone up in Kenya at the moment, so some people find it really hard to put food on the table, especially those who earn below the dollar. It's very hard for them to survive at the moment (Kenya);

✧ [the] agony of seeing a large number of people living in acute poverty, [who] are barely able to make ends meet and [who] have to survive on less than a dollar on [a] daily basis. In a country that is well-endowed with natural resources, it is unthinkable that in the midst of plenty many can suffer (Zambia);

✧ a great teacher that taught us to be strong, persevere in faith and be steadfast in trials. Our church has been formed in trials (Bolivia);

> ✧ be[ing] compassionate ... with [other] people, to feel what
> they feel, to feel their pain and to try to do something
> about it like Jesus did in the Gospels (Palestine/Jordan).

Suffering is a tangible reality across our global church – poverty, war, loss of hope, division and natural disasters lead to great suffering. As God's chosen people, together, we are to both be mindful of and share in one another's sufferings. We are to have compassion for those who are suffering and listen to one another in our vastly different sufferings as we imitate and follow the suffering Christ, our chief shepherd. In 1 Peter 4, there are at least two actions that Peter commends to mitigate suffering: mutual, familial love and hospitality. In this reflection, we will talk about what suffering and hospitality might mean in our own contexts. Just like Christians today, the recipients of 1 Peter suffer. In chapter 4, Peter goes to the heart of what suffering means for the Christian community.

Discussion Part One: Contexts

To ground this reflection, we begin by engaging with a conversation between three of our brothers and sisters – Moderator Azad Marshall from the Church of Pakistan, Diocese of Raiwind; Bishop Justin Duckworth from the Diocese of Wellington in New Zealand; and Mama Claudaline Muhindo, widow of Bishop Désiré Kadhoro, Diocese of Goma in the Democratic Republic of the Congo. Together they discuss what it means to suffer as God's holy people in God's church and God's world and within their own contexts. The following paragraphs set out the beginning of their discussion.

Bishop Justin Duckworth introduces himself as the Bishop of the Diocese of Wellington, which is a central diocese in Aotearoa, New Zealand. Wellington City is the capital city and also the most secular city in the world for people between the ages of 15 and 45 – that is, Wellington City has more people who profess no religious faith per capita than anywhere else in the world. Bishop Justin expresses his feeling that this is a very exciting place to be because he is dealing with people who now in the West have no concept of the gospel and who have grown up in a context in which they have been 'inoculated' to the good news of Jesus. These are people who have, in many senses, seen the gospel as connected with colonization, patriarchy and numerous other parts of an oppressive regime that many want to leave behind in New Zealand's history. Unfortunately, though, we are the church and we are a church that is part of that history. So, Bishop Justin thinks that, until we can take responsibility and in some sense repent of this history, it will be a 'blockage' of the gospel in Wellington. While he wants to call this suffering, he recognizes it as probably a humbling that has taken place as well, as the church in New Zealand is no longer as prominent as it was in the past.

Bishop Azad Marshall introduces himself as the Moderator or the president-bishop for the Church of Pakistan. It is his 28th year of consecration. In Pakistan, he serves the Diocese of Raiwind, a very small and poor diocese where people have various needs and where many other issues of persecution and hardship are present as well. When he looks at 1 Peter chapter four, he notes that it 'seems as if it's written for us', with no 2,000 years difference. It seems as if everything that Peter is talking about is still happening today. The focus of Bishop Azad's ministry is social justice in Pakistan and confronting detrimental laws. Peter, in the first verse of chapter five, says he was an eyewitness and then he talks about his own suffering, so when we read 1 Peter, Bishop Azad notes, we are really listening to the Word of God in the first century from the Apostles who really suffered for Christ. In a way, this echoes the context in which Bishop Azad lives and works.

Muhindo Mogaroca Claudaline introduces herself as the widow of the late Désiré Mukanirwa, Bishop of the Anglican Diocese of Goma, Democratic Republic of the Congo (DRC). She still lives in the DRC, in the same diocese in Goma. After Bishop Désiré's death, she says, the community was so … 'persecuted'. This was not easy for them, particularly as it was so difficult to accept Bishop Désiré's death and come to terms with the fact that they were left alone to live their lives without him. By God's grace, though, they are still here and continue to be here.

From Mama Claudaline's point of view, she had worked with Bishop Désiré in the pastoral ministry of Jesus Christ from the beginning. This pastoral and episcopal ministry was complicated and not so easy, due to surrounding tribal conflicts and misunderstandings among Christians, [God's] servants, themselves. Sometimes, she notes, we think that to be in Jesus Christ is to be at peace, to eat and to drink, but it is not: it is about suffering. We suffer day and night. There are burdens that we have to carry and there are people who target us. Through this conversation, we come to understand that to be in Jesus Christ is to suffer in Jesus Christ.

'Following Jesus means suffering with Jesus', says Mama Claudaline. I Peter 4 'seems as if it's written for us', says Moderator Azad. Just like Christians today, the recipients of 1 Peter suffer. In chapter 4, Peter goes to the heart of what suffering means for the Christian community. His starting point is this: 'Christ suffered in the flesh', and just as 'Christ suffered in the flesh', so Peter's community is to suffer 'also with the same intention' (4.1).

That 'Christ suffered in the flesh' is not, however, a call to death and martyrdom. 'Christ's sufferings' certainly include his Passion and death on the cross, but throughout his ministry Jesus experienced hostility, mockery and rejection by his closest associates. He experienced economic vulnerability as well as physical pain. Many turned against him because he embraced those excluded and marginalized. Believers should therefore not be 'surprised' by their sufferings (4.12). That the community suffers should not come as a shock, 'as though something strange were happening' to the community (4.12). Suffering is for the name of Christ. But, addressing Christians with little power, Peter locates their unjust sufferings in the context of Christian hope. Christ's glory is still *to be revealed*, and that glory is a beacon towards which his community is called to orient their lives. Suffering will not have the last word.

This hope for the future does not, however, exempt Christians from acting and doing good 'now'. Peter's focus in chapter 4 has thus far been primarily on what believers are not to do, with a list of behaviours they are to leave behind. Now, Peter reminds this community what is required of them, beginning with 'constant love for one another' (4.8). This love isn't just for the sake of the individual or for salvation: the purpose of love here is inclusion and unity, 'for love covers a multitude of sins' (4.8). With the theme of God's judgement fresh on readers' minds, the Christian community is called, when faced with sin and the behaviour of non-believers, not to judge but to love. This is a love rooted in the forgiveness and love of God, and such language echoes the call in the opening chapter of this letter to 'have genuine mutual love, [to] love one another deeply from the heart' (1.22).

This is the kind of love that will define the Christian community and enable it to avoid the malice, slander, resentment and strife that arise when we fail to forgive. But love is not the only action in which believers are called to engage, for 1 Peter 4.9 introduces another essential element of communal life: hospitality without grumbling. Here is a brief set of reflections on how we might understand hospitality today.

Excursus: Voices on Hospitality

In my context, hospitality is:

✧ sharing the little we have with other needy people. We say in Chichewa, '*Kakudia, skachepa*', meaning food is never too small to share (Zambia);

✧ just accepting people and welcoming them as they are and for what they are (Sri Lanka);

✧ sharing food and sharing place and sharing shelter and sharing whatever you have with brothers and sisters, especially those who come to us as pilgrims in the land of the Holy One (Israel);

✧ opening your entire being to listen, opening your arms to welcome and love, opening your homes to offer a warm space, preparing your table to bless the hungry, kneeling in prayer with the sick – that's hospitality for me (Guyana);

✧ cultivating relationships in your life with family, with friends, with strangers and creating a welcoming space to be (Canada);

✧ by the grace of God welcoming a stranger, a person that I may not know as such, and giving him or her that welcome, as though I'm welcoming Christ Jesus (South Sudan/United Kingdom);

✧ welcoming strangers as if they were friends, which is actually quite hard to do, but even more than that it's about being their guest [and] recognizing that I need to go to their less familiar places rather than always expecting them to come to mine (United Kingdom);

✧ welcoming people home and cooking lots and lots of food for them (India);

✧ in the Bedouin tradition, it has a very special meaning, where the guest is protected by the host. So, in the Bedouin's hospitality, the guest is protected totally from any harm. The guest is also given a refuge and a patronage, and at the same time is given freedom. They'll never ask a guest 'what is the reason [for] your visit?' before three days pass (Palestine);

✧ that I must learn to live simply so that I have enough and more to share with those in need (Sri Lanka);

✧ a kind of welcoming people who are in need, welcoming them in your heart by sharing with them the pain that they are going through and pray[ing] for them and also go[ing] with them the same suffering that they are going through. You have to feel as [if] you are the very person who is also going through that suffering (South Sudan);

✧ sharing our resources with someone who needs it and using whatever gifts or talents that we have to serve those in need (Malaysia);

✧ even during the pandemic: 'Food Always In This Home', F-A-I-T-H. Whoever was travelling by, they said: 'Come, whoever you are, come and have food and go. Come and have some water and go' (India/Germany);

✧ a hallmark in Ghanaian community, that despite the unfavourable economic situation in Ghana, many Ghanaians see hospitality as a sacred duty. The flip side for me [is that] hospitality is not just receiving people to entertain, but [is] welcoming people for who they are. But this way gradually is eroding from our society or from our consciousness I grew up in a society where everyone is accepted, but now people want to attack people. It's about who I get on with, who I agree with, and that makes us less hospitable. That is a challenge, and I want to see hospitality from this perspective, not just coexisting. It's not just trying

> to tolerate people but celebrating people. I want to cele-
> brate my brothers and sisters, bishops in the Anglican
> Communion, celebrating them, celebrating their cultures,
> celebrating their worldviews, celebrating their challenges,
> celebrating their gains and everything. That is, for me,
> hospitality (Ghana).

Much more than toleration and coexistence, hospitality is care, welcome, compassion, listening, creating space and protecting the vulnerable. The Greek word for 'hospitality' is literally 'love of stranger', which is a fascinating call for those who are 'aliens and exiles'. Because they share the same alienation from the world, they must offer a welcoming home for one another. And, just as those who are aliens and exiles have been given an identity as God's chosen people, so too does hospitality change the identity of those who offer and receive it. They are no longer strangers.

Hospitality involves risk. It makes us vulnerable. Some of the greatest hostility Jesus faced was when he restored others and shared a meal with them, when he offered and received hospitality. Peter makes clear, however, that we do not have to – indeed we cannot – do this by our own strength. Christ and the grace of God remain absolutely central. We acknowledge our dependence on God, and when we do so, we credit God for what he accomplishes through us and we pray it might honour and glorify him 'through Jesus Christ' (4.11).

Peter calls all to offer hospitality and support to fellow Christians who face suffering and persecution for their faith, so that we may be drawn together, not pulled apart, in our diverse and shared sufferings. This text calls all, especially those who might be suffering less, to move toward those who are suffering and to support them with genuine love and hospitality. We may think particularly today of suffering for Jesus' name. Others might ridicule us as Christians, trying to shame those who are associated with the name of Christ, but this ridicule, for Peter, is an opportunity to honour the God who made the shameful cross a throne of victory. The God who makes the unholy holy will vindicate those who bear Christ's name.

The chapter returns, then, not only to the suffering of Christ as the pattern for Christian suffering, but also to the assurance that God is a just judge who will ultimately make things right. Even in the midst of suffering, the foundation of our hope is in God, who will not fail us. Loving one another and being hospitable is not always easy. We like to grumble, especially when such love impinges on the resources and the gifts we have been given. But all we have is grace. Let us engage once again with three of our brothers and sisters in Christ on hospitality and suffering in their diverse contexts.

Discussion Part Two: Testimony on Hospitality and Suffering

Bishop Azad notes that hospitality takes many different forms, and that the church in Pakistan is known for offering quality education to the larger community. Most of their schools have a majority of the students from the Muslim faith, but the church has always been at the forefront of educating the whole nation. In the first 30 years of Pakistan as a nation, Christian schools were the only schools offering a good, quality education. Not only that, but, like the medical hospitals when refugees were coming into Pakistan from the Indian side, it was the Christians who were there to look after them. The church in Pakistan is not an inward-looking church. Bishop Azad recognizes that his diocese and the church have problems, persecution and difficulties in so many ways because of the laws in Pakistan and the relationship of the church to the government, but he affirms that the church has not given up on doing what it has been asked through the Scriptures.

Bishop Justin believes the forgotten art in the West is hospitality, and he therefore thinks it is and has been incredibly significant in and, in a sense, the backbone of his ministry. He reflects that hospitality has become a lot more difficult since he has become a bishop because of the regional nature of this ministry and the necessity of travelling a lot more. It is, therefore, much harder to be present and harder to practise hospitality as a bishop.

Mama Claudaline describes hospitality in her diocesan context as a necessity for Christians and servants of God despite the pain they live through in the service of God. For example, in our churches, she says, there are many people who need us. People who suffer outnumber people who are well-off, and so hospitality means thinking about the people who are suffering. What can we do for them? We must be with them, even those who are not Christians. They need our hospitality. Even Jesus Christ, in his life on earth, showed hospitality, not only towards his own disciples, but also towards all those who needed him. That is why hospitality is a key element in Mama Claudaline's ministry. She says that we must demonstrate God's love, we must help others and we must help them to feel the love of God. The gospel ... comes with hospitality.

Mama Claudaline then recounts something she once said to her husband: 'Go ahead with church evangelism, church planting, peace and reconciliation issues in the church, but my vocation is to take care of those who are most vulnerable, most in need.' She notes, however, that she 'would say materially, but unfortunately [she] can't afford it'. This was Mama Claudaline's role with her husband when he served in the church. She took care of people who were in need, taught them skills and worked on health and schooling issues for children.

Bishop Azad recollects that, when he was a bishop in Iran, there were hardly any priests left. He says that he likes to share the stories of how people suffer, and so with great difficulty he discovered that there was only one priest left in Iran. Bishop Azad remembers that his visit to this last priest was a beautiful expression of how God's people have survived the worst kind of suffering, not just anywhere or only in our own contexts, but right in the Anglican Communion, because Iran is part of the Anglican Communion. When Bishop Azad went to see him, he remembers that this priest told him that he was imprisoned, tortured and, when he was released, was told he was not allowed to go near his church. This priest said: 'I long to really go back to my work and work as a priest, but I tell you something: let me show you my chapel.' And so, sharing a small house with his son, he took me [to] a little room, ten by ten, which was like a store, and he had converted that into his chapel where he had hung his cassock, his tape recorder, his prayer book, his Bible, all these things. Then he said: 'This is my chapel, and I come here every day and I pray for Iran and I pray that God will allow the church in Iran to be open again. I have never stopped praying for my church in all these years of persecution and difficulties, [even] when I am not allowed to serve openly ... will you please help me and talk to the government?' Bishop Azad says this is another story, but that they got permission for him to start working again. Until this priest died he continued to serve in his old age, serving his congregation in Isfahan. There are people whose lives have changed because they recognize their challenges and see that they are something. For Bishop Azad, it is special to know what makes people stay faithful when they suffer. He posits that it is the wonderful grace that God gives us to be able to deal with our situations, so that, through the

lives of our dear brothers, [God] is glorified even in the
middle of the very hard circumstances. That is hospitality
and the compassion that the church is known to offer to
the world, and without complaining. There is so much to
learn from our dear brothers and sisters who are in [diffi-
cult] situations.

Bishop Justin reflects on his own context after listening
to Mama Claudaline and Bishop Azad, wondering whether
he and other Christians ... somehow believe that the kingdom will come without us joining in Christ's suffering, or
whether we can 'get the kingdom coming' without participating in suffering. In his own life, he and his wife have for
many years been very committed to hospitality, and they
have had numerous people living with them. They raised
their family in the context of having former inmates living
with them, and he acknowledges there have been some
risks, though he stops short of calling it suffering. They
have had their car stolen and crashed – kind of a minor
example, he notes – but he thinks that, because of their
hospitality to the stranger, they have benefited more and
been blessed more in some senses. He feels like hospitality has enriched their lives, despite the 'inconvenience' of
constantly trying to find room for one more. The challenge
Bishop Justin singles out in his context is related to the
passage from 1 Peter in which Peter speaks of hospitality
as meaning hospitality to the stranger, because he thinks
that we are often in our church context actually giving
hospitality to each other and not to the stranger. He thinks
this challenges us to minister to those who are different
[from] us and to those we do not know. A second challenge
he identifies is not just us giving hospitality but having
the humility to receive hospitality from the stranger as
well. That is what Jesus did. Jesus came into our world,

and chose to visit with us as strangers, and humbled himself and made himself vulnerable. Bishop Justin says this is what he is thinking deeply about and taking away from the conversation.

Mama Claudaline concludes, after hearing from her 'fellow brothers', with the recognition of the risks that come with the ministry of hospitality. She says that we need to show hospitality to others and give hospitality in the church of Christ, but that, by being hospitable, we encounter many risks. She is sure that each of us would have much to say about the problems we have encountered in the ministry of hospitality, and so, she says: 'Hospitality, this gift we get from God, which we use in the church, has never been without difficulties, without suffering in Christ.'

Mama Claudaline encourages us to take courage, and all our panellists call us to give God control. Even though things may be difficult, there is victory.

Conclusion

As we have just read, hospitality and suffering often go hand in hand. Hospitality is especially an issue for Christian leaders and their families because of those who come to their door. While it may not be the same as suffering, ministry has a cost – whether an economic cost, a cost of privacy or a cost of vulnerability. Hospitality calls us to be with those who are not like us. It is the opposite of the security of exclusion, but there is also great power and privilege in hospitality.

There is power in saying 'no' and refusing to extend love, refusing to share that with which we have been blessed. Wherever there is power there is room for abuse and for exclusion.

Think of the refugees in our world who do not receive hospitality and welcome from some of the wealthiest nations on earth – nations that often identify as Christian. Think of the Covid vaccine, and the refusal to share it. Think of the way our economic systems exploit the most vulnerable people in the poorest places while the richest grow richer. We export suffering to our brothers and sisters to benefit ourselves. We are good at creating crises but not very good at compassion for those who face the consequences. As more and more people are literally exiled from their land and driven from their homes and jobs due to the growing climate emergency, the call to offer hospitality – literally, to *welcome the stranger* – is ever present and, in many places, a matter of life and death.

Exporting suffering makes us numb. It hardens our hearts to our brothers and sisters and it hardens our hearts to God. The powerful need to be hospitable to suffering, to *import* suffering. That means sacrifice, be it money or power. It means the powerful willingly becoming less comfortable – in terms of racial reconciliation and conversation, trade, employment, prices, vaccines and economic power generally – in order to lift the weight of suffering from others. How as the global church do we maintain love and offer hospitality, given that suffering looks very different in different parts of our world? How do we offer Christ hospitality, and imitate Christ in our hospitality?

Questions for Bible Study

Suffering: Write down two or three things that come to mind when you think of the word 'suffering'.

Reflect on the following questions:
✧ When you hear the word 'suffering', what image comes to your mind?
✧ What emotion(s) does it stir in you?

Suffering and Community: Think about your community – either your faith community or wider social context.

Reflect on the following questions:
✧ What are your community's beliefs about suffering?
✧ For example, are you told to accept suffering because it is the will of God? Is there an assumption that being a 'good' Christian will protect you from suffering? Are there other beliefs about suffering in your community?
✧ If you are in a group, how does understanding of suffering differ across contexts and communities?

Suffering and Joy: 1 Peter 4.12–16: 'Beloved, do not be surprised at the fiery ordeal that is taking place among you to test you, as though something strange were happening to you. But rejoice in so far as you are sharing Christ's sufferings, so that you may also be glad and shout for joy when his glory is revealed. If you are reviled for the name of Christ, you are blessed, because the spirit of glory, which is the Spirit of God, is resting on you. But let none of you suffer as a murderer, a thief, a criminal, or even as a mischief-maker. Yet if any of you suffers as a Christian, do not consider it a disgrace, but glorify God because you bear this name.'

Reflect on the following questions:

✧ What do you hear 1 Peter saying about suffering that might be similar or different to your own view or that of your faith community?

✧ Within your context, what does it mean to rejoice in the face of suffering?

Suffering and Hospitality: All of 1 Peter's advice directs us toward the 'other' or the 'stranger', especially when we realize that the Greek word for 'hospitality' means 'love of the stranger'. 1 Peter 4.8–10: 'Above all, maintain constant love for one another, for love covers a multitude of sins. Be hospitable to one another without complaining. Like good stewards of the manifold grace of God, serve one another with whatever gift each of you has received.'

Reflect on the following questions:

✧ What does constant love and hospitality in the face of suffering look like in your context?

✧ How are you called to give and receive hospitality in your community and wider society, especially with those who are on the margins?

5

Authority in Christ

1 Peter 5

Within 1 Peter 5, we encounter the 'roaring lion' who 'prowls about, looking for someone to devour' (5.8). This final reflection begins with global voices describing the 'roaring lion' in their contexts.

Excursus: Voices on the Roaring Lion

In my context, the roaring lion is:

✧ the [reality] I cannot get used to: injustice. I faced a lot of injustice in my land, in my country, personally in my family and seeing many others suffering from injustice. Crossing a checkpoint is humiliating and that's injustice. I faced it, I lived all my life under occupation, but I cannot get used to injustice. That's a cry, that's a call to do something about it. Not to take revenge, but to practise the commandment of love towards everyone, especially those who suffer from injustice (Palestine/Jordan);

✧ the suffering caused by war and displacement, and this has created brokenness, anxiety, trauma and sometimes loneliness and isolation (South Sudan/United Kingdom);

✧ [that,] in Ghana, road accidents are on the increase, [as well as] armed robbery [and] the astronomic fuel prices (Ghana);

✧ [the reality] that has the capacity to seek to devour where I am, the church and what it stands for, is a kind of aggressive un-thought-out secularism. I am always willing to engage in robust intellectual arguments, but we certainly experience here a kind of aggressive ill-thought-out secularism which wants to diminish and even silence the church's intelligent attempts to make a contribution to the public square, and to me the roaring lion is an attitude that is very prevalent around me, which suggests that Christian voice in society is not just unintelligent but actually dangerous (Ireland);

✧ corruption and plunder of national resources. Ultimately this perpetuates poverty, and makes the poor poorer and the rich richer (Zambia);

✧ for asylum seekers in Cyprus, loss of hope (Cyprus);

✧ occupation. Occupation unfortunately drives people from their homes and pushes people from their land, from their olive trees, from their history, from their culture (Israel);

✧ fear (Kenya);

✧ [what] we're living in at the moment: a time when leaders appear to be roaring lions from what I see, and I think of the roaring lion as somebody who abuses their position of leadership and power for selfish ambition (United Kingdom);

✧ indifference (Uruguay);

✧ the devil himself, who comes to destroy and steal and kill, so when he sees that people are in unity he comes in and scatter[s] people and make[s] people leave the place and not live in harmony and in oneness (South Sudan);

✧ the ruling government, [which] is actively playing on the side of roaring lion by allowing persecutions, withdrawing benefits over conversion, etc. (India);

✧ colonialism, new colonialism, unchecked capitalism [and] all forms of domination [and] subjugation would be a roaring lion that threatens not only our lives but our humanity (Palestine);

✧ [something that] spells danger from someone in power who can do whatever they like, even to the extent of manipulating and using others for their own gain (Malaysia);

✧ corruption. The quest for what does not belong to you – be it power, be it property, be it purse, whatever – now that's the roaring lion that is gnawing the very fabric of society today. Now corruption devours creation (India/Germany);

✧ an individualistic culture that focuses on hustling and always doing more. It's focused on achieving and what benefits me as an individual and putting relationships on the back burner, or neglecting them completely (Canada);

✧ [that] recently we had a target killing of one of our lay pastors [in Pakistan] because the ISIS that used to be in Iraq and Syria, they have shifted to Afghanistan. So the wave of terrorism has entered into Pakistan. It is a roaring lion for us which really shakes the people whom we look after and we work with. This is a roaring lion for us (Pakistan).

Exposition of 1 Peter 5

There are significant and terrifying lions in our world. These lions are the devil, powerful and evil. So often, when we read 1 Peter, we do not get to the lions. In many of our readings of 1 Peter 5 and especially in relation to leadership, we stop with the call to be a shepherd. That is, however, not how this letter works. This chapter unpacks for us what the call of a shepherd and of the whole community under their care really entails.

If being a good shepherd is about tending the flock, then resisting the lions roaming around seeking to devour the sheep is at the heart of the job description. Peter is clear that our proper stance toward this lion is watchful, clear-headed resistance. The command is to 'keep alert' (1 Pet. 5.8); there is no option for laziness or complacency. A key, core part of being a good shepherd is resisting the adversary, the roaring lion. But what are the roaring lions of injustice in our communities? Who – or what – is the adversary? For contemporary Christians in the global church, those forces that stand for all that is evil are numerous and should be named, as they have been in the testimonies we have engaged above. We have, in previous reflections, considered the tendency to tell those who are suffering to keep quiet and to endure. Jesus' radical call in this final chapter of 1 Peter is to confront the lions, to resist the adversary and to protect the flock. So what does it mean to be a shepherd in 1 Peter, and how does that relate to our understandings of being shepherds to God's flock? Let's return once again to global voices and testimonies on shepherds in their contexts and experience.

Excursus: Voices on the Shepherd

In my context, the shepherd is:

✧ one who speaks with and for the poor, a promoter as well as protector of justice and human dignity, those that will move from their comfort zones and be where it matters most, among the least, among the common (Zambia);

✧ the one who extends his soul, a shoulder for me [so] that I can cry on it ... in time[s] of suffering, and in time[s] of disturbance and in time[s] of real atrocities. A shepherd is one who can really embrace me, and the shepherd is one whose presence and whose nearness enables me for a sound sleep (Pakistan);

✧ [one who] cares for the flock through ringing the bell, summoning the faithful to prayer and worship. He prays for them and for their healing, he feeds himself from the Word of God and feeds others (Argentina);

✧ someone who gives his life in order to protect others (South Sudan);

✧ [one] who knows the people, who has counsel for the people, [who is] loving, caring and praying for the people. A shepherd should have an exemplary life (India);

✧ that auntie in church who you know, if you're going the wrong way, she is going to say something about it (Trinidad);

✧ although we can't often change the future for them, enabling others to recognize that they have the gifts to accompany asylum-seekers a little on their journey, to make the time that they have in Cyprus a better one (Cyprus);

✧ want[ing] to leave the 99 sheep and go after the one lost sheep. [A shepherd] tells me that everybody matter[s] (Ghana);

✧ [those like] a couple of clergy [I can think of] who particularly during the war time [when] mass groups of people were displaced could have, if they wanted to, use[d] their power to escape [but they] chose to move with their communities throughout the displacement areas, so they went into camps, they went into areas that were not very well-resourced to be in solidarity with their parish, with the people who didn't have the power to escape that conflict (Sri Lanka);

✧ a person who has a prophetic voice in the midst of challenge, in the midst of difficult times (Israel);

> ✧ my pastor, who led me to Christ in the days of my youth, and to me he has been a good shepherd who has walked with me all through my faith, and up until this day he has been following [up with] me. One of my sisters says he was like a walking Jesus, and indeed he was like a walking Jesus. He would reach out to me in my lows and in my highs, and he would always have that booming smile on him and he was someone that the love of Christ and the light of Christ radiates in him (South Sudan/United Kingdom).

Continued Reflection on 1 Peter 5

'A shepherd is like a walking Jesus who radiates the love of Christ.' 1 Peter was written before ministry was solidified into the three-fold order of bishop, presbyter and deacon. Unlike other New Testament writings, 1 Peter does not use the noun 'bishop' (*episkopos*). Instead, 1 Peter prefers the term 'elder' (*presbyter*), a neutral term that can refer to both female and male elders. This term designates those within the congregation who are older, and possibly those who are older in the faith as well. Peter calls himself a 'fellow elder', rather than an apostle, teacher or spiritual father. In choosing the same title as those to whom he is writing, Peter signals his common cause with them. He writes to them as one of them, exhorting them as a fellow elder rather than commanding them as one in authority.

The verb 'to shepherd' echoes the command to Peter at the end of John's Gospel to shepherd and nurture the flock of Jesus. It calls to mind Jesus' own teaching about the nature of the 'good shepherd' in John 10.1–18: one who lays down his life for the flock, whose sheep know his voice, who knows his sheep by name and who leads his sheep out to pasture. The shepherd is also the one who searches for the lost sheep, who is both pastor and evangelist. This is a call to a demotion rather than a promotion within the ancient world.

Shepherding also calls for relationship, which is what allows for flourishing. Peter follows this call to 'tend the flock' with three ways that such shepherding should happen. First, the shepherding is not to be done by compulsion, nor for gain, nor by lording it over those in their charge. Shepherding the flock is to be undertaken willingly, eagerly and should set an example. Second, Peter takes the imitation of Christ one step further through the image of the shepherd. He calls the elders to be examples to the flock of the good shepherd who washes the feet of his disciples and challenges the injustice of the empire by laying down his life on behalf of his friends. The verb exhorting them to 'be examples' is better understood as 'becoming examples', which is active and a process. The elders must continue to learn and grow in order to be patterns for the rest of the believers. Ultimately, elders remain members of the flock, shepherded themselves by 'the chief shepherd'. They stand in a liminal space: they are both sheep and shepherd, both needing guidance and called to guide.

Only Christ is chief shepherd. Only God in Christ can help them know, name and resist the lions. The lion is all that seeks to kill and limit life for those in our world, all that seeks to reduce the quality of life. Finally, elders should also practise humility. Humility changes the face of power. Before God, all are humbled; no one is exalted, except by God's own actions. Peter's exhortation to humility echoes the teaching of Jesus in the Gospels: 'All who exalt themselves will be humbled, and all who humble themselves will be exalted' (Matt. 23.12). Peter immediately connects humility with the casting off of anxiety. Letting go of anxiety is an act of humility. Many translations read 'cast all your anxiety on him', but a more accurate translation is 'casting all your anxieties on him' (1 Pet. 5.7). Casting our anxieties on God is an act of humbling ourselves before God. We acknowledge that God has the strength and wisdom that we do not, and we entrust ourselves, our sufferings, to him over and over again.

Peter reminds the community that they do not face perse-cution alone. They are part of a persecuted community that spans the Roman Empire, and they are reminded of their soli-darity. Their unity in Christ overcomes all division and threat, even as they suffer. They do not suffer alone, nor do they resist alone. This letter balances the call to resilience in situations of vulnerability and marginalization, and the call to resistance from positions of power. Here, at the end of the letter, we are invited to join God in his activity of resistance in order to build community. In our world today, we need to take care not to imply that there is one right way to respond to suffering. The testimony of those in the midst of suffering is almost always different from those observing from the outside.

Conversation with Archbishop Jackson Ole Sapit

So, how do we protect the flock and keep alert? The role of a leader is to create unity, not division, because division makes the lion's job easier. Division makes it easy to pick off the weak and all those vulnerable to attack. One of our brothers in Christ has not only been a herdsboy in a place where there are lions threatening the flock, but he has also been part of two close encounters with lions. As you will learn from him, the lion is fought and defeated in situations of absolute confusion and chaos, but those taking on the lion are nevertheless united in their confusion. They are united in their chaos.

Unity is chaotic and can be confusing, because unity doesn't mean we all agree. But we are united in Christ. We are united against the lion. We are united in protecting God's flock, given to us. Unity is needed even in the midst of chaos – sometimes of our own making! – to defeat the roaring lion. So, we turn to a conversation that I (JW) had with Archbishop Jackson Ole Sapit (JOS).

JW   Archbishop, tell us a little bit about your upbringing, your family, your background.

JOS   Thank you, Your Grace, for welcoming me and for this interview. I was born in 1964 in a deep rural village in Narok, deep rural Kenya, next to the Maasai Mara, not so far away. And I was born to a large polygamous family, my father had 11 wives and my mother was number seven. They were not Christians and around 1969, when I was four years old, my father died.

In 1972, Archbishop Jackson, his mother and three sisters were sent away from his father's land by his step-brothers, losing their inheritance.

JOS   I ... my three sisters and my mother went back to where she was born. My sisters never had the opportunity to go to school and I went to school because the government [at] that time began to want to educate Maasai children, and there was a Chief's Act. The local chiefs were ordered by the government to bring children to school, so we were rounded up and taken to school. After getting into school, a year later, World Vision, a Christian organization, came to that village looking for children to sponsor. So, I became one of the first cohort of sponsored children in Kenya in 1975. I was a herds-boy and before we went to school, even after we went to school, [on] every school holiday we [would] be herding cattle and sheep and goats in turns.

     People in the village and young boys are trained from a very tender age how to herd cattle and how to live in the jungle ... These are jungles where you intermingle with the hyenas, with lions, with the cheetahs and leopards, buffaloes and elephants – everything is in the jungle with the Maasai and their livestock. As we grew up, part of the culture is to teach ourselves as young boys and young [men] how to become a strong warrior by fighting some of those tough animals. And I participated in a lion hunt and the Maasai expectation of every warrior

	is to participate and be part of a lion hunt and [be] lion killers. And I participated in two lion fights ...
JW	And would this be in daytime or nighttime?
JOS	Daytime, yes, you can't really fight a lion during the night because they see better at night and we don't, but during the days [is] when we hunt, and in one of them it was actually fatal because one of the young men was killed in my presence. I also have a lion scar in my left shoulder where, after spearing it ... [it] tried to grab me and then the claws got in, but never pulled me because he was going to fall down because of the spear, but I was lucky.
JW	Were you frightened when you went on that lion hunt?
JOS	Yes, the roaring of the lion is so, so frightening, but you know, you 'psych yourselves' as young people – you know how young people can psych themselves – until you are, like, there's nothing. And we used to tie bells around our thighs and we put some leaves on them so that they don't ring until we encircle the lion, and you go and when we spot the lion, we surround it and then all the boys will remove the leaves in the bells tied to their thighs and we begin making every bell ring, and that create[s] a noise that will confuse even the roaring of the lion. So, the boys will be yelling, their lion will be roaring, the bells will be ringing, so we fight in confusion, it was a very confused state; you realize what was happening afterwards. It is those [times] that you don't realize what was happening when you are in it, but you just go and realize when you begin to reflect about it.
JW	And it's extraordinary. We're reading the first letter of Peter, and it has that extraordinary, powerful passage in chapter five where he's talking to leaders and to young people and to the church as a whole and saying: 'Be alert, be sober, your enemy the devil, like a roaring lion, prowls around seeking whom to devour.' Now, when you hear that, what's the picture in your mind?

JOS   You know, there are those things you read sometimes
       and if you have no experience, you just pass the sen-
       tence. But as I read that passage and speaking of the
       roaring of the lion, [it] called to my mind the roaring of
       the lions we fought, and it's not just when you're fight-
       ing. Every night when you are living where the lions are,
       they will roar every night and in me it is so fresh. When
       I read that, I know what a lion roar means. You know,
       when it roar[s] near the house, everything shakes. You
       know, our houses are made of sticks and mud and you
       can hear, if there are utensils around, you can hear them
       shake because the voice is so deep and so intense, and it
       is very, very scary, especially when it roars and you are
       seeing it in front of you. And therefore when the Bible
       speaks of the devil roaring like a lion, I could now see
       the reality of the danger. God is warning us that unless
       we cling to him the world is a dangerous place.

JW   So, when you read this as a bishop, how does it affect
       the way you look at the world? Does it mean that you're
       simply looking out for danger or does it mean more than
       that? Because I'm very struck that as a young man you
       didn't only hear the lion, [but] you went out to find the
       lion and defeat it, so how does that work as a bishop?

JOS   Yes, shepherding is a big thing in my culture because
       you grow into it, and shepherding means many things. I
       remember when I was recruited to theological college as
       an ordinand, the bishop then, when he met me for the
       first time, asked me this question: 'Have you decided to
       leave your father's cows to come and study to shepherd
       people?' I said yes, [and] he said: 'Do you think it is the
       same, shepherding cows and shepherding people?' And
       I paused for a minute – I did not know where he was
       headed – and the kind of answer I gave, I don't know,
       I think God guided me. I said: 'Yes, the principles are
       the same because [when] shepherding animals you make
       sure that they are safe, you make sure that the sick are

treated, you also make sure that they have good pasture and they have water, and therefore you ensure they have provisions but you also ensure that they are protected.' And reading the letter of Peter, particularly chapter five, bring[s] to memory the way I answered that day, but now when I became bishop, it became more broad and more intense, because now I will see things differently.

[At] that time I had a narrower sense that is only preaching, praying for them, visiting the sick, going to their homes and ... doing pastoral care. That was my narrow sense, but my broader sense now is, looking at the extended environment, [to] protect them [and] make sure that they are food secure, so I have to challenge the nation on the agricultural policy because I care about food security; I care about national security and terror-ism that is happening in parts of Kenya because safety is a work of a shepherd. I care [about] recklessness among our political class and mismanagement of the economy because it affects people directly. I care about ecology and [the] environment because it affect[s] us in a bigger sense, in a broader sense, and therefore now my shep-herding is not just in that narrow village sense. I look at the global picture, the national picture. We are now talk-ing about the war in Ukraine. It's affecting everybody in the world; even Kenya is not unaffected by the same war because we get wheat from Ukraine.

JW   I suppose a further question: I was very struck, when we were all together looking at 1 Peter 5, [that] Peter talks about being a fellow elder. Who shepherds the shep-herds? How do the shepherds find a shepherd when they are tired and worn down? Who picks them up?

JOS   Yes, that speaks to me because I asked myself that ques-tion. Recently, I had my house of bishops and we are struggling [with] who shepherd[s] the bishop, because we are supposed to shepherd clergy. Then I ask[ed] 'who shepherd[s] the Archbishop?' We find ourselves very vulnerable in those spaces because people don't come near you sometimes unless you have opened up your heart, unless we are willing to be vulnerable before them, and therefore it's a big struggle to know who shepherd[s] the shepherds.

But my word of consolation to myself and to all of us is that we have the chief shepherd, Jesus Christ, our shepherd. If we rely on him and be humble before him, it makes [it] easier [for me] to come to you and lay bare my vulnerability, because God humbles. If I have a relationship with Jesus, I will be able to create a fellowship of people around us who can tell us when we are not doing right, who can show us what we don't know [and] who can enable us to see things we don't see, because sometimes this busy life block[s] our minds and our eyes to see even the most important things around ourselves, and I find myself in that position many times, that I'm so blinded by a busy life that I don't see the most important things around myself. And therefore we need God to show us who can give us support, because we are human and we are weak like everybody else and I think that's what we need to learn from Peter as a church and ask ourselves: 'Are we playing the elder's role? Are we humble enough? Are we showing by example? Do we show them what to do and how to do it?' And I think [that], when Peter is talking to himself as an elder among elders, he has reduced himself to the same level.

Conclusion

This conversation just recounted offers an astonishing reflection on the fear, the terror, the danger and the confusion that roaring lions create. The role of a shepherd is to be a leader, an exemplar, who is humble and finds their strength and hope in the chief shepherd. For, ultimately, the story of how to take on a roaring lion, of how to protect the flock, of how to lead as one of the elders is a story of unity and solidarity, even in the midst of confusion and chaos. *Unity in Christ overcomes all division and threat.*

Peter ends by returning once again to the central themes of hope, suffering and glory in Christ. His final call is one of reconciliation: to stay in relationship and stand in solidarity with brothers and sisters who are suffering. How will we shepherd differently after listening deeply to stories of suffering? How will we ensure we are in relationship and constantly being transformed into the likeness of our good, chief shepherd? How will we hold on to the encounter with one another and with God? Because without relationship, without encounter, issues arise. To resist the lions, all that threatens our flocks, we must remain in community. This isn't a one-off thing either; like so much of Peter's ethics, it is living and continuous, ongoing and transformative.

Peter also returns to the promise of the glory of Christ, who already has victory over the demonic, a cosmic victory over the lion, by his cross and resurrection. The shepherds are part of that resurrection victory. The call of the Christian, and the promise to the Christian, is to share the suffering and the resurrection and the glory of Christ. *This is good news.* The temporary nature of suffering is seen in the light of God's ever-lasting, eternal promise of salvation. At the end of the letter, the promise of what salvation entails is specific: called to 'eternal glory in Christ', God will 'restore, support, strengthen and establish you' (5.10). This is the God who takes on our anxieties, this is the God in whom Peter's followers must trust and this is the God to whom 'be power for ever and ever' (5.11). Whatever suffering is endured for Christ, God's promises revealed in Christ are eternal, assured and wonderful beyond all hope. The power and promises of God will always have the final word.

Questions for Bible Study

Shepherd: 1 Peter 5.1–4: 'Now as an elder myself and a witness of the sufferings of Christ, as well as one who shares in the glory to be revealed, I exhort the elders among you to tend the flock of God that is in your charge, exercising the oversight, not under compulsion but willingly, as God would have you do it – not for sordid gain but eagerly. Do not lord it over those in your charge, but be examples to the flock. And when the chief shepherd appears, you will win the crown of glory that never fades away.'

Reflect on the following questions:

✧ What is your understanding of a shepherd?
✧ How should a shepherd lead according to 1 Peter?
✧ What does it mean to imitate Jesus as the 'chief shepherd'?

Humility: 1 Peter 5.5b–7: 'And all of you must clothe yourselves with humility in your dealings with one another, for "God opposes the proud, but gives grace to the humble." Humble yourselves therefore under the mighty hand of God, so that he may exalt you in due time. Cast all your anxiety on him, because he cares for you.'

Reflect on one or more of the following questions:

✧ What does it mean to clothe yourself with humility?
✧ How are humility and the casting of your anxiety on God connected?
✧ How do you practise humility in your life and ministry?

Roaring Lions: 1 Peter 5.8–9: 'Discipline yourselves, keep alert. Like a roaring lion your adversary the devil prowls around, looking for someone to devour. Resist him, steadfast in your faith, for you know that your brothers and sisters in all the world are undergoing the same kinds of suffering.'

Reflect on the following questions:
- ✧ Who or what are the roaring lions in your context? Who or what is threatening your community?
- ✧ In your context, how do you resist these lions?
- ✧ In your context, how do you keep steadfast in your faith?
- ✧ How might you support other brothers and sisters in the world who are suffering?
- ✧ What kind of support do you need in your ministry and faith?

Conclusion

JENNIFER STRAWBRIDGE AND
ABIGAIL HARRIES MARTIN

The words of 1 Peter give a better conclusion to these biblical expositions and studies than anything we can offer:

> [T]he God of all grace, who has called you to his eternal glory in Christ, will himself restore, support, strengthen, and establish you. To him be the power for ever and ever. Amen. (1 Pet. 5.10b–11)

Like living stones, precious in God's sight, go in peace to proclaim the mighty acts of God.

Final Reflections on 1 Peter

Introduction to the Reflections
from Archbishop Justin

In addition to the biblical reflections and Bible studies on 1 Peter offered above, the following section contains five shorter reflections on each chapter of 1 Peter by leading biblical theologians from across the world. These are homiletic in form and may be especially helpful for preachers who engage with 1 Peter through the lectionary or in a sermon series.

They were initially offered in Canterbury Cathedral, composed for the opening retreat for bishops at the Lambeth Conference in 2022, and they introduce some of the key challenges of 1 Peter for the church and her leaders today. The scholars represent a range of contexts, cultures and experiences, and include Isabelle Hamley from the United Kingdom and France, Paul Swarup from India, Esther Mombo from Kenya, Paulo Ueti from Brazil, and Jennifer Strawbridge from the United Kingdom and United States. Questions are included at the end of each reflection to support personal prayer or group conversation together.

The Anglican Communion is a family that spans the entire globe. We bring our vastly different experiences, contexts and backgrounds to our understandings of the themes in 1 Peter. In these reflections, I have encountered the text and the Lord afresh, been challenged by different perspectives, and blessed by new revelations of the greatness of God. I pray they might now be a gift to the wider church, a chance to recognize and celebrate our unity across our global diversity, to reflect in our own local contexts and to recognize how God's word speaks to us across time, distance and difference.

I want to express my immense thanks to Jenn, Abbie, Chris Russell, those who attended the St Augustine's seminars and to the gift that funded them from St Augustine's Foundation and to many more people. These global contributions enable us to find afresh the living power of God's word in the voices of different generations, nationalities, church traditions, gender and cultural backgrounds. Each voice challenges in very different ways, but the result is a book of exciting and refreshing insights, developments and above all that in the grace of God, through our Saviour and Lord Jesus Christ, and led by the Holy Spirit, we are being built together as living stones. May these readings of 1 Peter enable us afresh to proclaim the wonderful works of him who called us out of darkness into his marvellous light, and to love one another, for as Peter says (perhaps slightly ruefully), 'love covers a multitude of sins' (1 Pet. 4.8).

1 Peter 1

ISABELLE HAMLEY

We gather in the name of the God, who, in the words of 1 Peter, 'has given us a new birth into a living hope through the resurrection of Jesus Christ from the dead' (1.3). As we gather, we take time to place ourselves before God, and before one another.

And there is no better place to start than with the words of Peter. Peter is writing to 'the exiles of the Dispersion' (1 Pet. 1.1), to the people of God scattered and dispersed trying to live faithfully in a world full of challenges.

Take a moment now to look around yourself, and 'see' the people around you – gathered from scattered places, with different challenges, yet together today as the people of God, brought together to seek God, praise God and share the story of God.

The world we share is not much brighter than the world of Peter's readers. It is a world of violence and conflict, a world of inequality, and a world often hostile to those of faith. The question, for the people Peter was writing to, was, how do we live faithfully in this world? How do you engage? How do you nurture hope where there seems to be no hope?

Peter, however, does not start by answering these questions. Peter starts by reminding the churches of who God is, and of who they are; he reminds them of what God has done, and of who they are called to be – which is probably a good place for us to start. Reflecting on who God is, what God has done in our lives as individuals, as communities, as churches; and reflecting on who we are called to be.

So who is this God around whom we gather?

1 Peter says, 'Although you have not seen him, you love him; and even though you do not see him now, you believe in him and rejoice with an indescribable and glorious joy' (1.8). First and foremost, the letter puts before us a reminder of the work of Jesus Christ. It reminds us that God acts first: God's grace has been extended to us, and invited us in. Before we can even think of what we might do, how we inhabit the world, we acknowledge that God has loved us first, and offered us grace. And we know God because he is revealed in Jesus Christ.

Wherever we have come from, whatever we have brought with us, we are gathered here because each and every one of us has been called by the Lord Jesus Christ.

Like Peter's readers, we have not seen him. But we love him. It is worth pausing here and asking, why do we love him? Who is this Jesus that you love and follow?

God reveals himself to the church: when we come together, somehow, our vision is expanded; by listening to the stories of many others, our understanding of God is stretched and expanded, we can be challenged, comforted and encouraged. It is as a church that we are called to know God, and when we gather together like this, when we share and listen carefully, we can come to know God more deeply. As we share stories of God at work, we can nurture vision and hope together.

In 1 Peter, the picture of who God is and what God has done inspires readers to trust and hope; it places the present moment in between memory and promise, between the memory of what God has already done, and the promise of his presence and transformation for the future. This in-between place, our present, is therefore a dynamic place, a place where God can be at work today, in ways that we can trust, because they have been both demonstrated in the past and promised for the future. Peter's picture of the work of God invites us to place our own story and stories within the great sweep of God's story.

As we do this, we invite God to come in and transform our own stories. The invitation, as it were, is mutual. God invites us into relationship, but we also have to invite God into our lives, and open them up. And that is usually where the trouble starts – because to invite God in means to open ourselves to be challenged, transformed and reshaped.

Transformation here starts with the idea of new birth, of a completely new identity, a new sense of belonging, a transformation of how we see the world around us. New birth might evoke different images to all of us, depending on where we have come from. And there are lots of different things we could read from it – a new identity, new culture, new ways of being taught to us as we grow. But here, I want to draw on just one thread: that birth brings us into a family; a child cannot grow on their own, and their very being is dependent on the kindness, care and guidance of the rest of the family or community. In many ways, it is no different for Christians. Here, new birth is associated with a call to distinctive living, a call to holiness. This is the culture of the family of faith. Christians can only flourish within the context of the household of faith, so that their distinctiveness is embodied through the community's relationships.

See Peter's words:

Now that you have purified your souls by your obedience to the truth so that you have genuine mutual love, love one another deeply from the heart. (1 Pet. 1.22)

New birth, truth and distinctiveness have a clear outworking: genuine, deep mutual love. The people of God, in Peter, are called to hope and to holiness. And one of the ways in which these things are both nurtured and expressed is through the quality of life of the community of faith. Through deep and genuine mutual love.

What does this look like for us today? How can we bear the marks of deep and genuine mutual love for one another?

We are called to love one another. In 1 Peter, calling is not individualistic or personal only; it is the calling of the church as a whole. When the community loves, hope is nurtured, and holiness can flourish. When the community loves, it can begin to embody an alternative to the destructive ways of the Roman empire; when the community loves, those who struggle, those who are oppressed and diminished can learn to see themselves as God's people, holy and dearly loved.

But of course, love is probably the hardest thing for human beings to practise with a community of people called by God, rather than chosen by one another. Christian writer Eugene Peterson puts it this way:

And yet I decide, every day, to set aside what I can do best and attempt what I do very clumsily--open myself to the frustrations and failures of loving, daring to believe that failing in love is better than succeeding in pride. (Peterson, 2000, pp. 77–8)

Our efforts are always feeble; but in the life of the people of God, we live in between memory and promise, and we know that learning to love is not just born of our own efforts, but the work of the Spirit within us.

Questions for Reflection

1 Who is this Jesus whom you love?

2 What has God done in your life and the life of your community in the past that gives you hope?

3 Who is God calling you and your community to be?

References

Peterson, Eugene H., 2000, *A Long Obedience in the Same Direction: Discipleship in an Instant Society*, 2nd edn, Downers Grove, IL: InterVarsity Press.

1 Peter 2.1–12

The Church was chosen by God for God's World, and within 1 Peter 2 we are reassured about our living hope and our inheritance. Peter encourages us that testing our faith will show its *genuineness*. We are privileged because we know Christ and what he has done. We are called to be holy as he is holy. We are to be different from the world. We are to be alert and self-controlled to disable the attacks of the evil one. We are to be obedient. We are to remember that God is just and will judge us impartially. We cannot claim to know God yet walk in sin, thinking we are immune to judgement. Christ has paid the redemption for us by his shed blood on the cross, and purchased us to be slaves of Christ. Believers experience new birth and are to be transformed into Christ likeness. We are to love one another deeply to show our love for God in our community. We are to grow up in our salvation by eliminating all evil habits and craving pure spiritual milk. I would like us to focus on three main verbs in 1 Peter 2.1–12:

1 **Grow up** in your salvation.
2 **Come** to the living stone and be built up.
3 **Know** who you are – God's Church in God's World.

1 Grow up in your salvation – 1 Peter 2.1–3

Peter begins with encouragement to grow up in our salvation in two ways: Firstly, rid ourselves of ingrained habits that destroy the community. Peter lists five: malice, deceit, hypocrisy, envy and slander. We could add many more, but Peter considered these to be prominent. We should examine some of our ingrained habits that cause strife and broken relationships in our community and the world.

Secondly, Peter also calls us to crave *pure spiritual milk* like newborn babies, not that we remain spiritual babies but crave spiritual growth like a baby instinctively and frequently craves milk. Spiritual craving is a longing to be nurtured, to have a more intimate knowledge of the Lord's character and to experience him through his word and his Spirit so that we mature. God in Christ alone both conceives and sustains new birth. But we need to put off our attitudes and behaviours that are inconsistent with our new life and put on Christ.

2 Come to the living stone – be built into a spiritual house – 1 Peter 2.4–8

Peter reminds us that we have come to the Living Stone, Jesus who is also the Corner Stone, the essential foundation block that holds the building steady.

Peter creatively transposes Old Testament messianic stone texts to Jesus and the new reality inaugurated by his resurrection. Stone imagery in Judaism describes the anticipated Messiah, and Jesus applied it to himself (Matt. 21.42) – the stone people rejected became the Corner Stone.

A stone or rock metaphor is a *double entendre*, representing strength and reliability to those who trust God's work, but destruction to those who do not, for on this stone Jerusalem's residents stumble and are broken (Isa. 8.13–15; 28.16–17). What does this metaphor of Jesus as the Corner Stone mean to us? Is He the stone we trust? Or is He a stumbling block?

The Son of God's death was not an unthinkable defeat for him or God's kingdom. Rather by the cross and resurrection, God's eternal purpose of salvation was fulfilled. The crucifiers had accomplished what God's 'power and will had decided beforehand should happen' (Acts 4.28, NIV). Ironically, the builders who rejected Christ put God's Stone in place. Likewise, God's Church will experience suffering and rejection but will eventually accomplish God's purposes.

How do we see ourselves as followers of a rejected Messiah who had to suffer to accomplish his purposes? How should we respond to suffering, rejection and persecution for the sake of the Gospel?

3 Know who you are – God's Church in God's World – 1 Peter 2.9–10

Peter quotes Exodus 19.5–6, though in a different order, and applies it to Christians. He also adds two phrases, 'a chosen people' (γένος ἐκλεκτόν; 1 Pet. 2.9) and 'the people of God' (λαὸς θεοῦ; 1 Pet. 2.10).

A chosen people

With election comes ethical responsibility, and we see ethics and mission interlinked in Abraham's call in Genesis 18.19: 'For I have chosen him, so that he will direct his children and his household after him to keep the way of the Lord by doing what is right and just, so that the Lord will bring about for Abraham what he has promised him.' This choosing is Election; doing what is just and right is Ethics; and bringing people blessing is Mission. Abraham's descendants, the Israelite nation, were chosen to reveal Yahweh by their ethical lifestyle. As God's Church we are also chosen to lead ethical lives so the mission of God will be accomplished.

Three identity-defining Hebrew words given to the Israelites in Exodus 19.5–6 are applied to God's Church:

Segullah – A treasured possession: belonging to God
Kohenim – A priesthood: representing God to the people and bringing the people to God
Qadosh – A holy nation: being distinctive, different

How are we to understand this threefold identity and our role in God's World?

A treasured possession: In Hebrew 'treasured possession' is *segullah*, meaning a valued personal item and belonging. God calling Israel his treasured possession means Israel fully belongs to him. The picture is like a mother clasping her new-born close to her heart. God's responsibility is nurturing and protecting Israel who is close to his heart, but they are accountable to obey his commands. God's Church is also God's *segullah*. We belong to God, and we are accountable to him.

A royal priesthood: The second identifying phrase for Israel is 'a kingdom of priests' – *mamlekheth kohenim*. A priest's primary role is representing God to the people and bringing the people to God. But what is a nation of priests? In the Old Testament, a priest was a mediator in both directions between God and the people. He represented God both in his person and example (see Lev. 21.22), especially in his teaching (Deut. 33.10; Hos. 4.6; Mal. 2.4–7), and he brought people to God by interceding for them. The priests made the word and will of God known and also blessed the people in God's name. Israel as a nation of priests similarly represents God and his ways to humankind in their national life. As God's Church we are also to bring God to humankind by teaching his word, interceding and being a blessing to others.

Israel functions as God's holy priesthood when they live according to God's law of freedom, justice, love and compassion among the nations and for the nations. Similarly, God's people are to live such radical ethical and spiritual lives that we function as God's priesthood for God's world.

A holy nation: The third identifying phrase is that Israel is a holy nation – *goi kadosh*. 'Holy' means distinct from other people. Historically Israel is unique because Yahweh delivered them from Egyptian bondage. They are also to be religiously distinct, to have no other gods or idols, and no compromises or additions from other nations in their practices. Further, the Israelites are to be ethical, just and moral so others will see Yahweh's character reflected in them.

God has always called his people for the sake of the world. Throughout Old Testament history and today this calling hasn't been characterized by human faithfulness to God, but God's faithfulness to humanity. Through the sinless life of Jesus God fulfils both sides of the covenant. We as his disciples, as God's Church, are caught up in his vocation and achievement, and continue to be agents of blessing to God's world.

The people of God

God has called us from darkness to light to be people of the light. We belong to God in a special relationship that is a privilege and a responsibility. As recipients of God's mercy, we are to let people see our good deeds and glorify God.

Let us be reminded that we need to grow in our salvation. Let us get rid of malice, deceit, hypocrisy, envy, and slander and crave the pure spiritual milk of knowing God intimately and feed regularly and instinctively on his word. Let us be built into God's temple on his living Corner Stone because this tested stone will never let us down.

Let us know who we are – a chosen people, a treasured possession, a priestly kingdom, a holy nation – and bless God's World by introducing him, interceding, being spiritually and ethically distinct and people of light. Let us truly be God's Church for God's World.

Questions for Reflection

1 What behavioural patterns does Peter highlight that cause division and destroy relationships in the community? How can we get rid of them and grow in our salvation?

2 If the Church is built on the rejected corner stone, how should we cope with suffering and rejection by the world?

3 How does our identity as God's chosen people, treasured possession, kingdom of priests and holy nation affect the way we live as God's Church in God's world?

1 Peter 2.13 – 3.22

ESTHER MOMBO AND GODFREY ADERA[1]

Reflection Theme: There is a hole in our bucket – prefacing the dialogue on church and world affairs as continuous and unending

We gather with the central theme prayer and reflection, fellowship and dialogue on church and world affairs. To preface my reflection on this theme, allow me to remind you of a classic nursery rhyme 'There is a hole in my bucket'. Various versions exist but they differ only slightly, all describing a 'deadlock' situation. I will use a version commonly used among children in East Africa.

There's a hole in my bucket,
dear mother, dear mother,
there's a hole in my bucket,
dear mother, a hole.

Then mend it, dear daughter,
dear daughter, dear daughter,
then mend it, dear daughter,
and dear mother, mend it.

---

1 Godfrey Adera is a PhD student at St Paul's University, ordained in the Anglican Church of Kenya Maseno West diocese. Adera works with Esther Mombo as a researcher and Teaching Assistant and was instrumental in the research for this study.

This nursery school rhyme presents a protracted dialogue between two characters, a mother and a daughter, which culminates in a deadlock situation. The dialogue is necessitated by a leaking bucket. The mother's bucket leaks, so the daughter tells her to repair it.

As used metaphorically for this reflection, the bucket in this nursery rhyme refers to God's world, and the holes are the problems that affect our world today, which we are called to participate with 'mother creator' in fixing. This theme comes against the backdrop of a pandemic that has not only ravaged the economies of the world, but also exacerbated inequalities in access to healthcare, and inequalities in race, gender and social class in monstrous proportions. As if this is not enough, many of us here have come from places that are experiencing weather extremes such as long droughts or floods or mudslides and many more issues from mother nature.

The dialogue 'a hole in my bucket' offers a unique way of prefacing our theme from 1 Peter: prayer and reflection, fellowship and dialogue on church and world affairs. It reminds us of three very important things in this kind of a discourse:

1 That there is a 'hole' in the bucket, that is to say, there is a situation that needs redress.
2 That there are several key players that come into the dialogue with interests and varied perspectives. These players, though distinct in their identities and contextual backgrounds/social location, are related, if only because of the bucket.
3 We must be watchful of attitudes and postures of heart that may lead to deadlock in this kind of engagement. The efforts towards repairs demand mutuality and collaboration and calls for humility and openness, to learn from each other in the process.

It is the second and third points that provide the main thrust of our focus today. While the dialogue 'a hole in my bucket' offers the premises for reflection and dialogue, the epistle of 1 Peter 2.13–3.22 offers the content for our reflection. It shows vividly that the 'hole in the bucket' is brokenness in the world today.

There is a hole in the bucket: the poor, the outcast, the women, those with no rights, suffer most from this hole – the brokenness in the world – and those who are lowest in the hierarchy/world order are also made responsible to fix it, to save the water.

Most of us may agree that there is brokenness in our world today, but not everyone responds in the same manner. Yet, as church, our self-understanding – as God's called people, fashioned along with all humanity in God's likeness – demands that we not only identify the different characters in this broken world, but also hold each other accountable for repairing the breech.

The brokenness of the world emanates from broken human relationships from its most basic to complex forms. The context of 1 Peter 2.13—3.22 provides five kinds of relationships premised on the fact that broken human relationships lead to a broken world. These include:

1 Citizens and governments (2.13–17).
2 Employees and employers (2.18–25).
3 Husbands and wives/ men and women (3.1–7).
4 The believer and their neighbours (3.8–14).
5 The believer and God (3.15–22).

Fixing the Hole: the four Rs – Recognize, Repent, Redeem and Restore

There is a pattern in this healing of broken relationships as written in 1 Peter, starting with 3.8: 'Finally, all of you, have unity of spirit, sympathy, love for one another, a tender heart, and a humble mind.'

This verse demonstrates how hierarchy can be turned upside down: instead of ruling you should serve in solidarity. Humble, compassionate, loving, sympathetic, like-minded: all of you, both men and women, enslaved and freed, employers and employees.

Is this cocktail of virtues the answer to the hole in our bucket? At least it is presented as the answer, a holistic answer, different from our perception of how to fix a hole, how to fix the global problems in this world. It starts with relationality, with solidarity.

Lesson from the Rhyme

The mother begins by stating the obvious: there is a hole in the bucket. To fix the leaking bucket, the mother needs straw, to cut the straw, she needs a knife, to use the knife, she needs to sharpen it. But the sharpening stone must be damp, so she needs water. But to fetch water, she needs the bucket, yet the bucket has a hole in it.

Recognize – acknowledge the bucket is leaking and needs mending

Firstly, we should recognize what is broken in our world and name the systems and structures that contribute to its perpetuation. Our complicity in perpetuating the spread of the virus of hegemony in all its manifestations: racial injustice, capitalism and economic inequalities; and sexual and gender-based violence to name but a few.

Repent

When confronted by the brokenness in this world, many of us revert to the values and attitudes of the religious elite, as in the parable of the Good Samaritan. Having recognized the fact of brokenness, the Pharisee, teacher of the law, and ... all sought to distance themselves from the 'sin', by circumventing the problem. What they failed to realize was that their very attitudes served to convict them of complicity in a system that has no regard for the disenfranchized. That goes against God's expectations of us. Instead, God requires radical moves to realign the balances of power by recognizing the worth and dignity of all humanity. As an act of repentance, we acknowledge our complicity, and move toward redeeming the scales of justice and seeking redress for the victimized.

Redeem

In the book of Micah 6.8, we read the words: 'He has told you, O mortal, what is good; and what does the Lord require of you, but to do justice, and to love kindness and to walk humbly with your God?' The term 'justice' in this text refers either to retributive or restorative justice, or primarily focuses on the church's responsibility toward the most vulnerable among us. Justice must not only be realized through the *Missio Dei*; it must be seen and felt, just as the injustices were felt and seen by those who have been asphyxiated under the heels of religious hegemonies. It is thus good that the Archbishop of Canterbury spoke about the iconography of white Jesus, a while ago; this recognition is important and good for the church as a way of interrogating the colonial heritage, patriarchy and sexism in the church and culture. Perhaps the need to interrogate further what is in our religious and secular hegemonies that embody whiteness as norm.

Redress

The issues that we are called to deal with are not just social but they are issues of mission and we are to engage with them through the theological principles in the context of empire. The case in point is that of Zacchaeus the tax collector. He repented of his wicked ways and was willing to reimburse all that he had robbed from people with interest. I am aware of initiatives such as the Zacchaeus Project. The project calls for a global tax and economic system that acts like Zacchaeus' changed ways. It represents the visible 'proof' of our repentance and shows signs of the changes that are needed to our systems so that through the fruit of our work and wealth the poor are lifted up and those who have been exploited are recompensed. This applies to the global village, not just one part of the world.

Our Collective Response

The world is waiting and watching. It waits expectantly for a church that looks like the faith it professes. In the wake of Covid, conflict and climate change, there is much more work to be done to ensure that equal opportunities exist alongside equitable responses to the challenges we face. As the global Anglican Communion adopts 'Thy Kingdom Come', it may be worthwhile to ask: Whose kingdom – the church's, the empire's or God's?

Who is excluded and left for dead in a dis-united Kingdom, which fails to acknowledge and accept responsibility for the sins of its colonial past and continues to perpetuate the atrocities of racism, ableism and patriarchy? Where are the gaps? Where have we been immune to the cries of the victimized and marginalized? Have we been simply moving to the other side? How might we redeem and redress from our positions of privilege and power? For it is only then, that we can truly seek to repent with integrity as we strengthen our fellowship.

Questions for Reflection

1 As you consider the situation in your own context and in the global context:

   i What are the 'holes' in your contexts? Are they connected to the other contexts?

   ii What are some of the local remedies to the situation both in our local and global context?

2 As you think about walking, listening and witnessing together locally and globally:

   i Who are the key players in seeking for a solution in our local contexts?

   ii What are the barriers to an effective local and global corporation with other key players in dealing with the 'holes' in our contexts?

   iii From 1 Peter 3.8–9 how do we overcome these barriers as God's church as we witness in God's world?

1 Peter 4

PAULO UETI

I begin this meditation by invoking the Apostle Paul's message to the community of Philippians 2.3–8:

Nothing is to be done out of jealousy or vanity:
Instead, out of humility of mind
everyone should give preference to others,
Everyone pursuing not selfish interests but those of others.
Make your own the mind of Christ Jesus:
Who, being in the form of God, did not count equality
with God something to be grasped.
But he emptied himself, taking the form of a slave,
Becoming as human beings are;
And being in every way like a human being,
He was humbler yet, even to accepting death on a cross!
(NJB)

All of us have walked this Eastern path from Jerusalem to Emmaus and from Emmaus to Jerusalem according to Luke 24.13–35. This is a path of conversion, of revisiting our traumas, our false hopes, and of reimagining the world, community and mission, as Cleophas and his companion Mary did (Cleophas was married according to John 19.25). We are walking at each other's pace, actively listening to one another, supporting each other, praying and committing to our local contexts. We are here because we heard and answered God's call. We are devoted people. We decided to follow Jesus along his life path, a path where we also find suffering, bigotry and murder, and also new life and resurrection. We are blessed by the new meaning that suffering has in our spirituality and our daily lives. Suffering is no longer a condition to follow Jesus or a punishment for something done. We suffer like Christ did, but we do so 'for Christ, with Christ, and in Christ', which instead of tearing us down and destroying us, strengthens us and brings us together in one movement of love, grace and solidarity that affronts powers and reigns over death; that affronts our own limitations.

We are not alone. Even when our suffering derives from the fact that we are people who profess a Christian faith, we are accompanied by a strange companion: the Jesus of the walk to Emmaus who was expected to be a king like the others but who refused that image and position of privilege and instead presented himself as a servant, a friend, the suffering servant, as prophesied in Isaiah. The Jesus who was wrongfully accused based on false information, who was not entitled to a fair trial, who was savagely tortured, whose body, mind and spirit were abused, and who was eventually murdered by the oppressive powers of the Roman Empire with the blessing of religious leaders who believed in a complicit religious system of privilege and the ideo-theology of meritocracy. This companion named Jesus cares about us and our everyday lives. He wants to know what you are going through. He takes the initiative, comes close, and asks: 'What have you been discussing on the way?' What happened?

We, too, like the communities addressed in the Letter of Peter, are called to recognize the wounds he suffered and to be in solidarity with him: 'Since therefore Christ suffered in the flesh, arm yourselves also with the same intention (for whoever has suffered in the flesh has finished with sin), so as to live for the rest of your earthly life no longer by human desires but by the will of God' (1 Pet. 4.1–2). We recognize that we too are suffering the pains of this world and we are called to recognize our own pains, name them, share them with the community where we live, to love and serve. We are called to 'love one another' because of this.

Suffering must trigger empathy and solidarity. We must fight against the natural tendency towards isolation. The suffering of Jesus lived by the community is a cry of intense love to do something, to be instruments of healing and integration, to become whole again. We too, like the community to whom Peter speaks, like the couple on the road to Emmaus, are sad. We often put our heads down because of all the misery in this world of corruption, violence, isolation, selfishness, impotence, silencing. The Church too is sometimes silent in the face of the suffering of its members.

I would like to propose two minutes of silent personal reflection: What suffering have you experienced in your life, whether personally or in its wider context? When you are suffering and in pain, what are your needs? What do you want from the person standing next to you, from your family, from the church? Who do you know who is currently suffering?

Silence

According to the tradition of Genesis 1, when God spoke the earth happened. According to the tradition of Genesis 2, we human beings are made of elements that come from the earth: fertile soil and water. According to our biblical tradition and spirituality, God, we and the planet are deeply interconnected. Our common home is a sacrament, a sign, of the invisible presence of God and of his redeeming, restoring and liberating grace. But this home also suffers and wails and carries our sin of having forgotten to listen and walk as brothers and sisters with nature and all its elements. We transform nature, a source of life, into resources for our selfish interests of profit, exploitation and domination and not just to survive in harmony. Along the way, we forget to listen to the planet and to treat it like a brother who also needs affection, care and attention. We forget that we were called to 'till and keep' the planet (Gen. 2.15).

The suffering of Christ, which the community Peter addresses remembers and in which it recognizes itself, is a call to love unconditionally and to work collectively to live in abundance. The suffering of Christ is not a reason for resignation and stagnation. It is a call to be in solidarity with all those suffering, as well as with our planet that wails in pain and waits for redemption because God wants to make all things new.

According to the Letter of Paul to Timothy, God wants to save all people, regardless of race, skin colour, sexual orientation and practices, political orientation, economic status, gender, age, nationality, or religious background. And through baptism, we are all called to fulfil this mandate to save (heal, redress, greet, welcome and accompany) all people, as well as our planet, which suffers from the exploitation and extractive practices of oppressive groups.

We, the living sacrament of Jesus Crucified and Risen, the Church of God, are called to be a path of love, solidarity, healing and transformation for the people of God and for the world of God. We need to ask ourselves whether we are agents of grace or doom.

Like Peter's community, we too hear the call to make the experience of suffering a way of breaking with sin. Sin no longer has power over us because nothing can separate us from the love of God.

Chapter 4 of this letter invites us to:

- use our intelligence and wisdom to live in love and promote life;
- care for people in prayer and action;
- practise solidarity as a path of love and unity in Christ;
- be deacons for the world, for those who suffer the most, and to be caretakers of creation;
- put ourselves in the shoes of Jesus and be an extension of his ministry of healing and reconciliation, to be bridges instead of chains or anchors;
- exercise hospitality, first and foremost, as a requirement of Christian faith and spirituality.

I would like to end with a passage from the Letters of Peter and of John:

> Therefore, let those suffering in accordance with God's will entrust themselves to a faithful Creator, while continuing to do good. (1 Pet. 4.19)

> We know love by this, that he [Jesus Christ] laid down his life for us – and we ought to lay down our lives for one another. How does God's love abide in anyone who has the world's goods and sees a brother or sister in need and yet refuses help? Little children, let us love, not in word or speech, but in truth and action. (1 John 3.16–18)

Questions for Reflection

1 How can we be in solidarity with the people and planet who are suffering? What should we keep doing or start doing?

2 How are we proclaiming Jesus crucified as a path to healing, reconciliation and redemption from suffering?

---

1 Peter 5

JENNIFER STRAWBRIDGE

We are anxious. Anxiety is part of being human.

Some are anxious because, at any moment, the government could decide to close our church.

Some are anxious because the climate is changing and rivers have dried up, fire is a constant threat, and land is disappearing.

Some are anxious because we are surrounded by war, terror, occupation, people displaced from all that they know.

Some are anxious because we are targeted for the colour of our skin, the tribe of our birth, the person we love.

Some are anxious because we or someone we love are sick and have limited access to healthcare.

Humble yourselves therefore under the mighty hand of God, so that he may exalt you in due time. Cast all your anxiety on him, because he cares for you. (1 Pet. 5.6–7)

Scripture doesn't offer counsel for *if* anxiety happens. Scripture speaks to us about *when* anxiety happens. Everywhere we turn there are visible reminders of how much there is to be anxious about in our world and our lives. Reflect for a moment on an anxiety, a worry, that you are carrying.

Silence

Anxiety and suffering go hand in hand. So, too, do anxiety and loss of control. For 1 Peter, this was the very mark of his communities, called to imitate Christ who suffered, Christ who humbled himself to the Father. Suffering makes us anxious and the threat of suffering makes us anxious. The author of 1 Peter understands this connection: he senses his communities' anxieties in the midst of struggle, displacement and persecution. And so now, at the end of his letter, these communities are offered counsel as they continue to follow Christ, to enact constant, mutual love for one another, and to resist all that seeks to kill and to divide.

> *Humble yourselves therefore under the mighty hand of God, so that he may exalt you in due time. Cast all your anxiety on him, because he cares for you.* (1 Pet. 5.6–7)

Anxiety is contagious. Anxiety and fear often produce more anxiety and fear. We infect others with our anxiety; the anxiety that others carry impacts us. And when we are anxious, we have a lot of trouble remembering the God who is in control of our lives and our church. We have a lot of trouble remembering who it is that sustains us. We have a lot of trouble remembering that we are not alone.

Across Scripture, not just 1 Peter, we find wisdom concerning our anxiety. In the Psalms, we are told to 'Cast your burden on the Lord, and he will sustain you' (55.22). In the gospels, Jesus tells us not to 'worry about your life' (Matt. 6.25–34) and promises rest to those who are burdened (Matt. 11.27–28). 1 Peter doesn't say that those who follow Christ will never have anxiety or worry. Suffering is assumed for those who follow Christ. But 1 Peter does assure his readers that they can trust in God and God's promises – they can cast this anxiety onto him and humble themselves under his hand – because God's love and care endure. 1 Peter tells us time and again that we are not alone in the midst of our anxieties and that the one we follow, Jesus Christ, suffered as we suffer.

For was not anxiety among the pains that Jesus suffered as he prayed in the garden of Gethsemane sweating like drops of blood (Luke)? Was not anxiety one of the pains suffered by his followers when they locked themselves away in the upper room out of fear? 1 Peter promises that God is present with us in our suffering and anxiety; that brothers and sisters in Christ are in solidarity with us in suffering, but they do not take it away. They carry it with us and, in the case of our Lord, he redeems it.

Humble yourselves therefore under the mighty hand of God, so that he may exalt you in due time. Cast all your anxiety on him, because he cares for you. (1 Pet. 5.6–7)

What does casting our anxieties on God look like? In 1 Peter, this command is intimately connected with humility. In Greek, these words about anxiety and humility are one sentence. Be humble that God may exalt you; cast your anxiety on God because he cares for you are part of the same action in 1 Peter. The casting off of anxieties and clothing oneself with humility go hand in hand. One might even argue that casting our anxieties on God *is* an act of humility.

Humility requires self-awareness. It is not self-degrading or low self-regard. Rather, humility is related to *humus*, the word for earth or soil, it is related to the land, being grounded, to not thinking of ourselves as more important than our brothers and sisters in Christ. Humility in 1 Peter is set against pride.

And humility must always be considered in relationship to God. If pride is the original sin, in which we think we can be equal to God, can judge on God's behalf, and can know all that is good and evil, humility is what allows us to remember and recognize that God is God and we are not. Some early Christians, like the fourth-century bishop John Chrysostom, thought that humility was the key to Christian faith. Humility was, in his words, the 'mother, and root, and nurse, and foundation, and bond of all good things' (Homily 30 on the Acts of the Apostles).

Indeed, often when we examine our anxiety we realize that within our worrying is the presumption that we are in command; that somehow worrying about something will determine its outcome. And the more we engage with a worrisome thought, the more we trick ourselves into thinking we can control it. Casting off our anxieties, therefore, can feel like a daunting form of surrender. Truly letting go can leave us feeling empty-handed of the control we convinced ourselves we had.

Yet, such a reality, such a calling, to humility is an essential way that we are community together and how we support one another. When we suffer, when we struggle, we know more than ever that we are not in control and this can be terrifying and lead us into a spiral of anxiety. Such anxiety can both drive us inwards, cutting us off from our community, and such anxiety can lead to pride as we try to hold everything together by ourselves. In desperation, we often cast our anxieties onto others, rather than onto God. It can feel easier to point to groups and individuals who we believe guilty than to humble ourselves before God.

1 Peter, however, speaks of solidarity and of humility. He encourages us to let go of our pride and to have compassion, literally to suffer with one another, and be reminded time and again that God cares for us and wants to exalt us. We are called to spread humility and peace, rather than anxiety and division; to recognize each other in our common suffering and to allow this to bring us together in Christ, rather than wrench us apart within the fray of the world.

Offering our anxiety to God and clothing ourselves with humility are not actions that we do only once. Both are continuous acts. Just as 1 Peter calls us to be living stones, embracing a living hope, and being examples for our flocks, we cannot be complacent when it comes to our posture towards God. Casting our anxieties on God is something we are called to do over and over again. To trust God with all that we carry, with all that seeks to control us and all that we seek to control, reflects our posture toward God of humility. In the gospels, Jesus teaches that 'all who exalt themselves will be humbled and those who humble themselves will be exalted' (Luke 14.11) and calls his disciples to 'not worry about your life' (Matt. 6.25). To live under the mighty hand of God is to entrust ourselves, our suffering, our cares to God.

For 1 Peter reminds us that our call to follow Christ in his hope, his suffering, and his glory is not about us, but about God and God's actions. Before God, all are humbled and none are exalted except by God. 1 Peter reminds us time and again that in the midst of the anxieties we carry, God cares for us, blesses what the world refuses to bless, makes holy what the world deems unholy, loves what the world deems unlovable, and redeems what the world does not believe merits saving.

1 Peter concludes with a call not only to humility, but also to peace for 'all of you who are in Christ' (5.14). Both the peace and the love that this letter expresses occur in a time of persecution for the Church, at a time when the community is suffering, a time when the community and those who lead are anxious. What might such peace and love look like for us today as we follow Christ and seek to imitate him in his suffering, humility and sacrificial love? How do we trust that the God who takes on our anxiety is the same God to whom 'be power for ever and ever' (5.11).

Humble yourselves therefore under the mighty hand of God, so that he may exalt you in due time. Cast all your anxiety on him, because he cares for you. (1 Pet. 5.6–7)

How do we live as if God's promises to sustain, support, exalt and redeem us are our truth?

Questions for Reflection

1 What anxieties are you carrying right now? How might you offer these to the Lord?

2 How can we help and support our brothers and sisters in their anxieties?

3 How is casting your anxiety on God an act of humility? Where might you practise humility in your life? Your ministry?

4 In what ways does a spirit of humility benefit your church? Your community?

Printed in the USA
CPSIA information can be obtained
at www.ICGtesting.com
CBHW031219040524
7892CB00017B/61

9 780334 065647